Whats the Difference Between Anime and Manga?

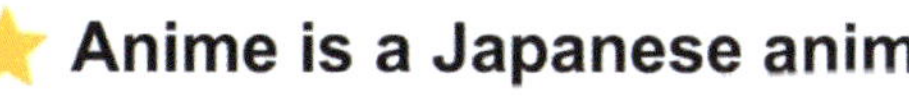

Anime is a Japanese animation.

Manga is Japanese drawn or printed art.

Anime and Manga's style of drawing are the same. They both have a strong range of art styles. They range from cartoon like to very artistic artwork. The characters you learn to draw in this book can be either Anime or Manga depending on how you use them. :D

NOTE: Before you go any further in this book I will be using the term Anime to mean both anime and manga for the duration of the book. I will be doing so for simplicity sake.

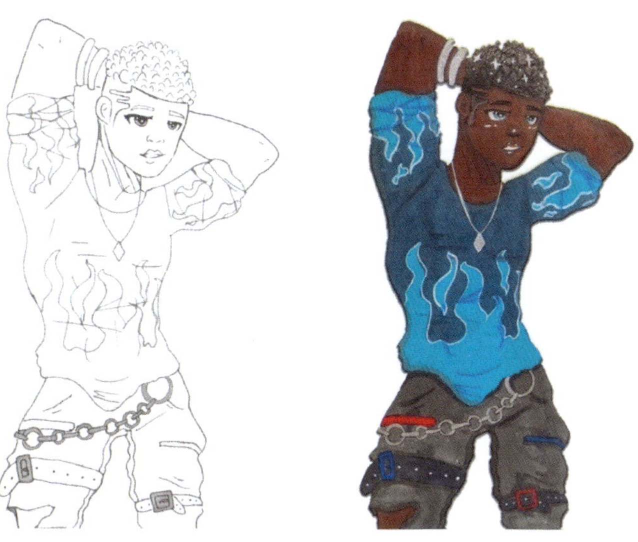

Materials

Of course you can start drawing anime with just basic paper and pencil. However here's a list of items that I use to create my anime drawings. Hopefully these items can Help you too! You can find all of these items on Amazon.

Hard Cover Sketchbook
A heavy duty water repellent hardcover will protect your paper from creasing. It's perfect for sketching, drawing and keeping your anime drawings organized.

Pencil
Any kind of pencil will do. Just make sure it's sharpened with a good eraser.

Charcoal Pencil
These pencils work great for blending and shading. They have more pigment than a regular pencil.

Colored Pencil
Great for blending, layering colors and shading .

18 or 48 Color fine point Drawing pen set
A vibrant pen set will help you add the details you need to make your anime drawings pop!

Alcohol Markers with Dual Tip
These vibrant pigmented markers are perfect for coloring your anime.

Alcohol Marker Colorless Blender
The colorless blender helps you blend alcohol marker colors perfectly.

Black Fine liner Micro Pens
Make sure you get the fine liner pens that are waterproof so they don't streak when you use your alcohol markers. These pens are great for outlining your pictures.

Fine Point White Gel Pens
These will help your drawings to look more professional. Great for creating the appearance of shine on your anime drawing.

Materials

Wooden Mannequin
The wooden mannequin is perfect for helping both beginner and advanced artist learn how to draw the human body in the right proportions.

Blender Stump
Blending stumps are great for blending and smoothing your pencil or charcoal drawings.

Kneaded Eraser
This eraser is perfect for any Artist. You can mold it into any shape to erase even the tiniest sections.
TIP: It also doubles as a stress ball, lol

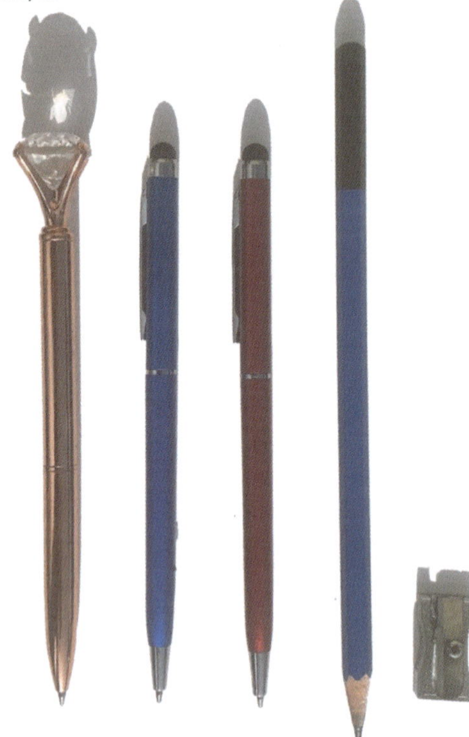

YOU HOLD THE KEYS TO YOUR SUCCESS!!!

Drawing Basics

In this chapter we will be covering the basics of drawing anime!
We will focus on how to sketch, shade and blend all together.
Let's get started!

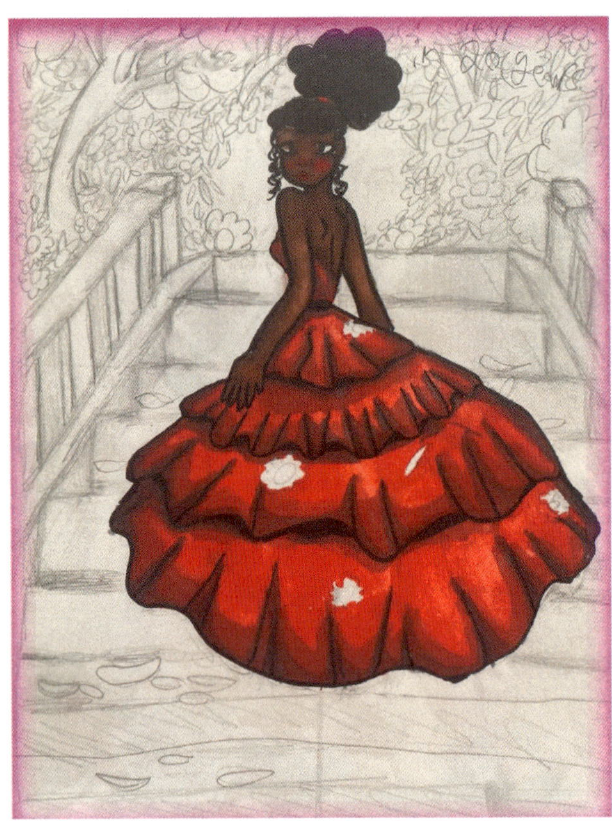

5 Basic Steps to Drawing Anime

The 5 basic steps to drawing anime are:

1. Create a basic structure of the face
2. Draw eyes and facial features
3. Draw the hair
4. Draw the body and add details
5. Add Color

Now that we've went over the 5 basic steps let's get started with shading!

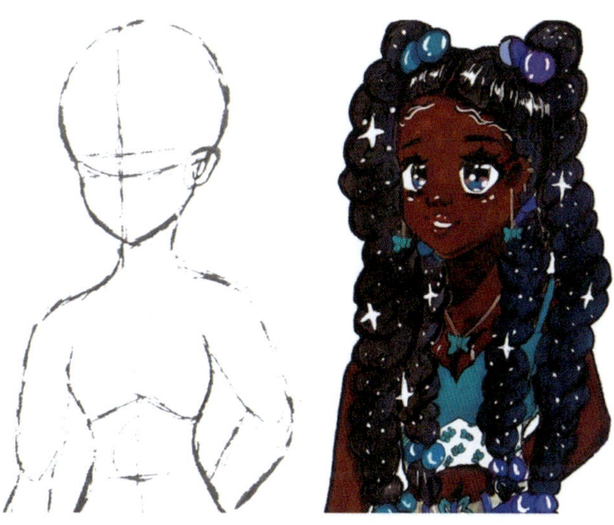

Types of Shading

Shading is the darkening or coloring of an illustration with parallel lines or a block of color. Shading can make your drawing look like a three dimensional solid object.

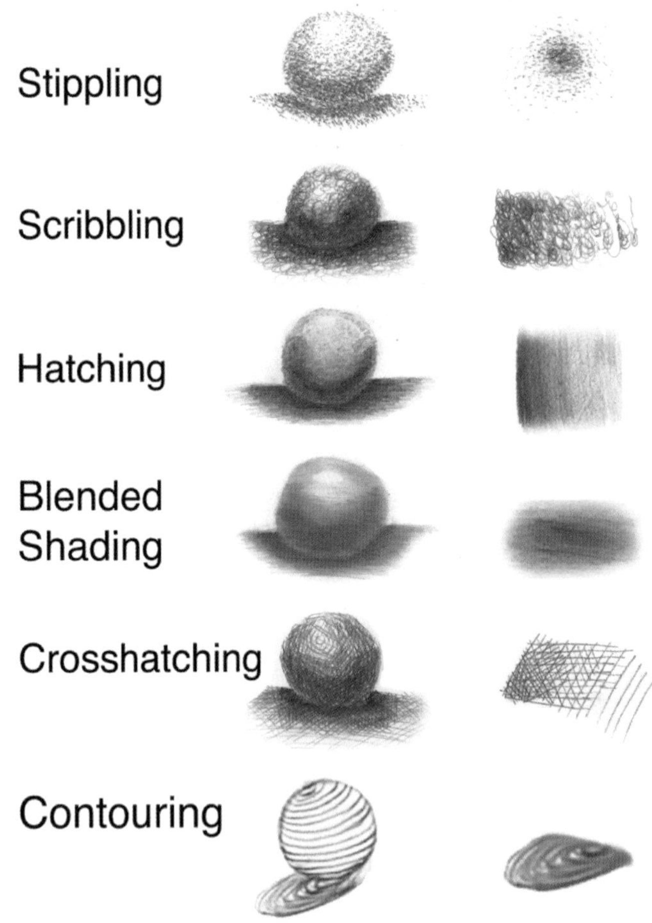

One of the most common types of shading and the one I use most is blended shading. Blended shading is simply a way to adjust the pressure you apply to the pencil on paper. Use a blending stump or tissue to lightly blend the shading. If you do this type of shading make sure you do it correctly. You don't want to see pencil lines!

Correct

Shade close together to fill up any white spaces to make a smooth blend. If you do this correctly you won't see lines.

Incorrect

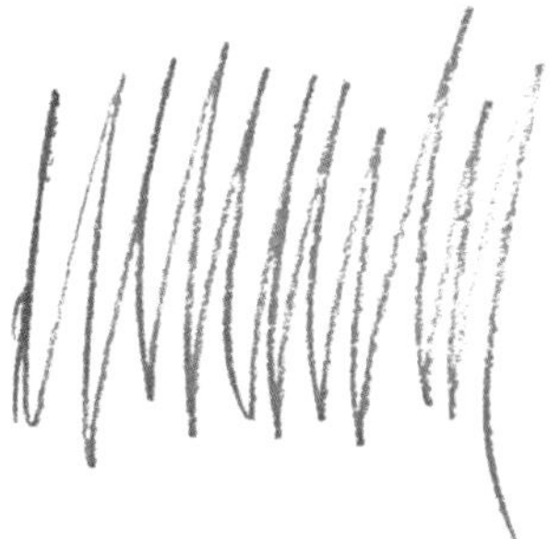

If you don't fill in the white spaces the blend won't look smooth. You will see the lines.

How to Blend

Look at the two lines below. The first line is shaded. You can see how many varations of the pencil shades I had to make to create this color scale. For the darkest color press your pencil down hard and shade. Gradually press your pencil with less pressure to get the lighter shades. The lightest shade should look white.

To blend the colors get a blending stick or a piece of tissue. Lightly rub the colors together until you notice them blending. A perfect blend should look like the second line below. You should not see the separation lines like in the first picture.

SHADED

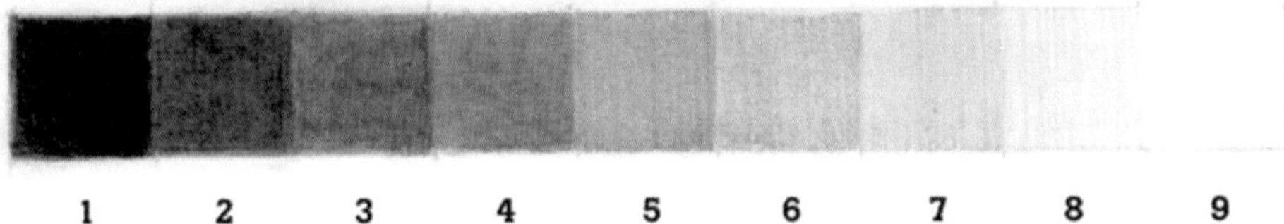

BLENDED

I used both shading and blending to draw this cupcake :)

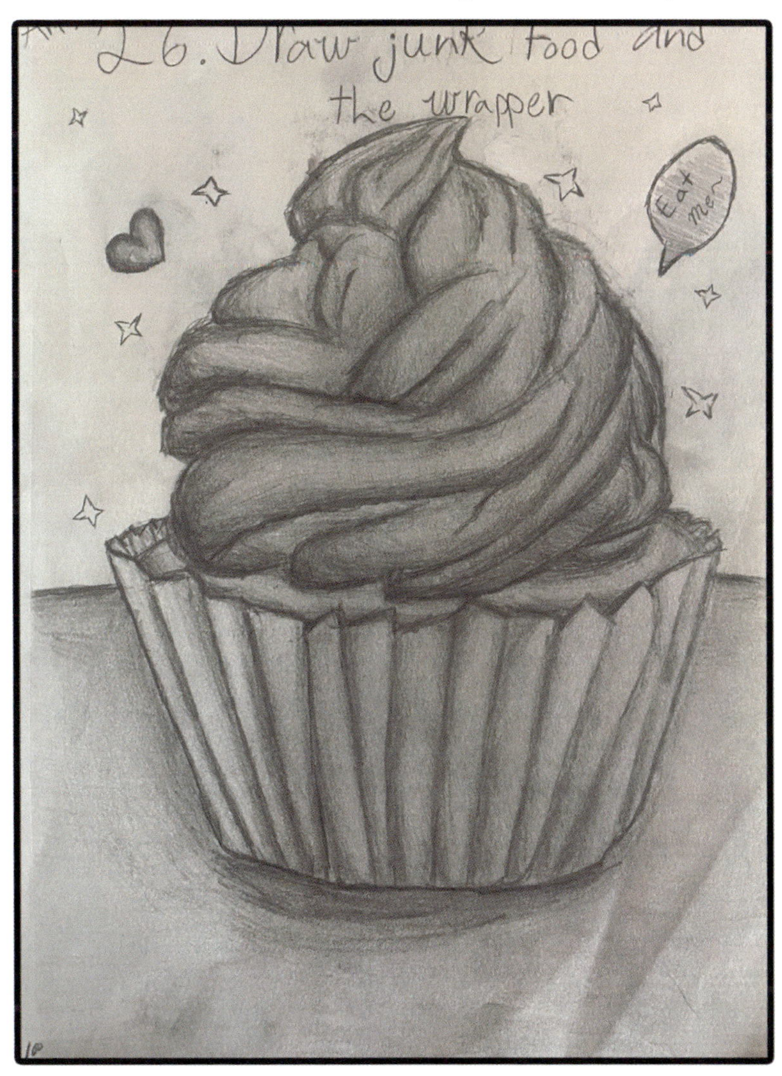

Blending with Alcohol Markers

Blending with alcohol markers is slightly different from blending with pencil. To create a perfect blend you will need a alcohol marker (colorless blender). It is possible to blend without the blender, but I prefer using the blender. For me it makes blending much easier.

Look at the picture below. The (Top) picture is how your blend should look if you do it correctly. The (bottom) picture is not the correct way.

CORRECT

INCORRECT

Down below I blended some colors together so you can see how well alcohol markers blend. I used the Ohuhu 120 marker set to create the blends below. Although their are several other sets you can choose from.

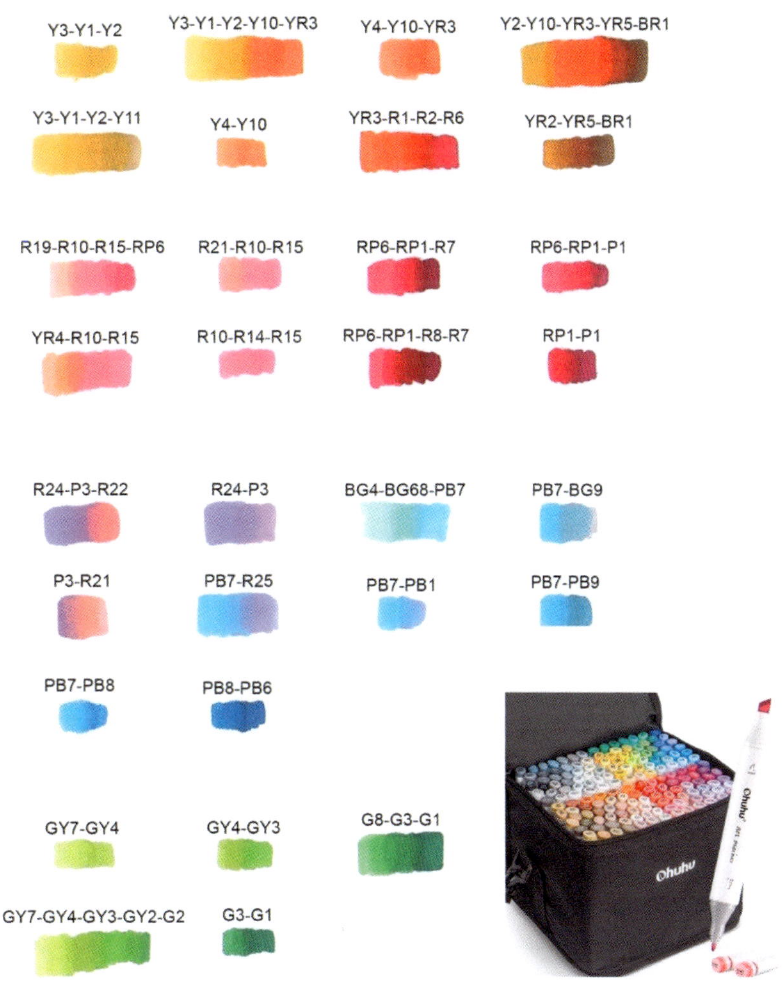

Light Source

When drawing anime some people like to add a light source and some do not. I find that adding a light source brings my drawings to life. If you plan to add a light source it's important to decide what part of your drawing will receive the light source and what part will be more in the shadows. Look at the cicles below each has a light source coming from a different direction. As you can see the area closest to the light source is lighter. It gradually gets darker the farther away from the light source you get. That is how you must shade your drawings.

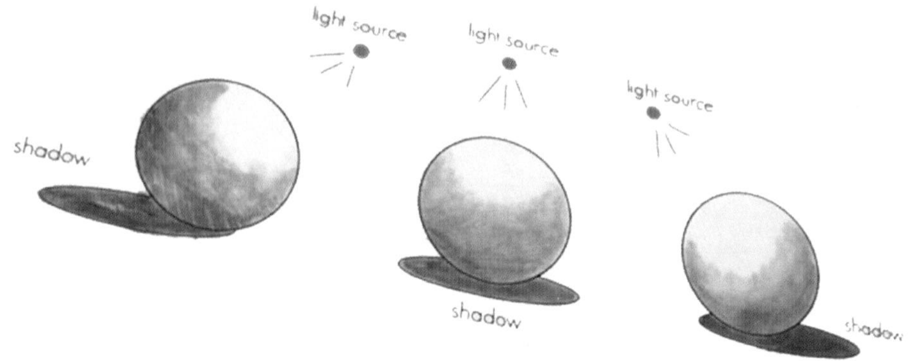

Shadows

Shadows are the areas on an object that receive little or no light. When drawing your anime you can use any of the shading techniques you learned in the earlier chapters to create the shadow. Below you can see how the different objects cast a shadow onto the surface.

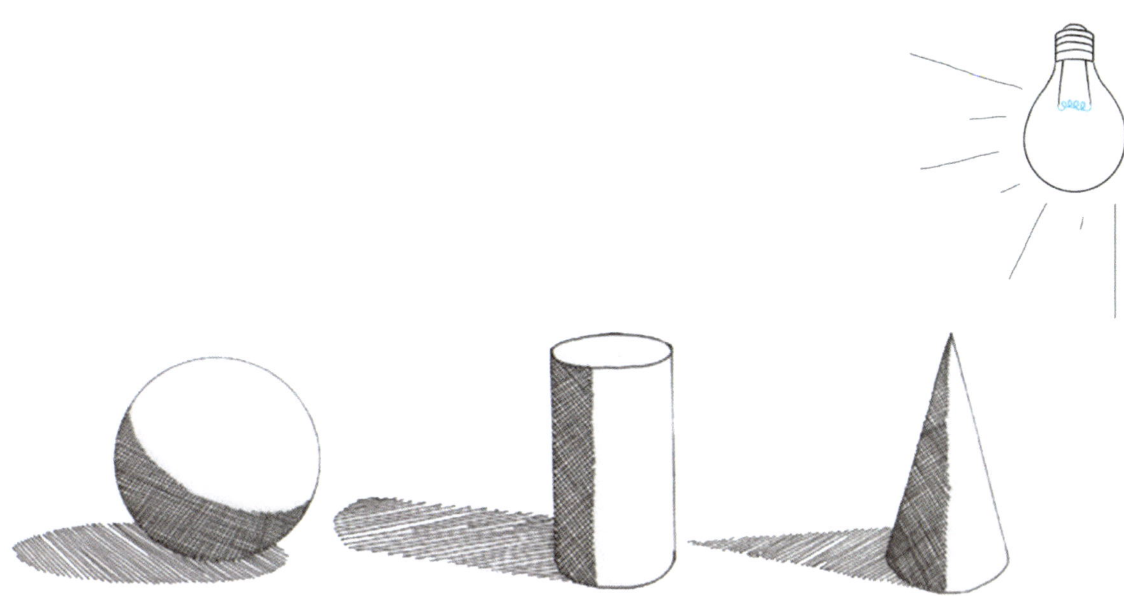

The shadow will appear different depending on what type of object or texture it is hitting. Notice below how I added shadow to my characters face and clothing.

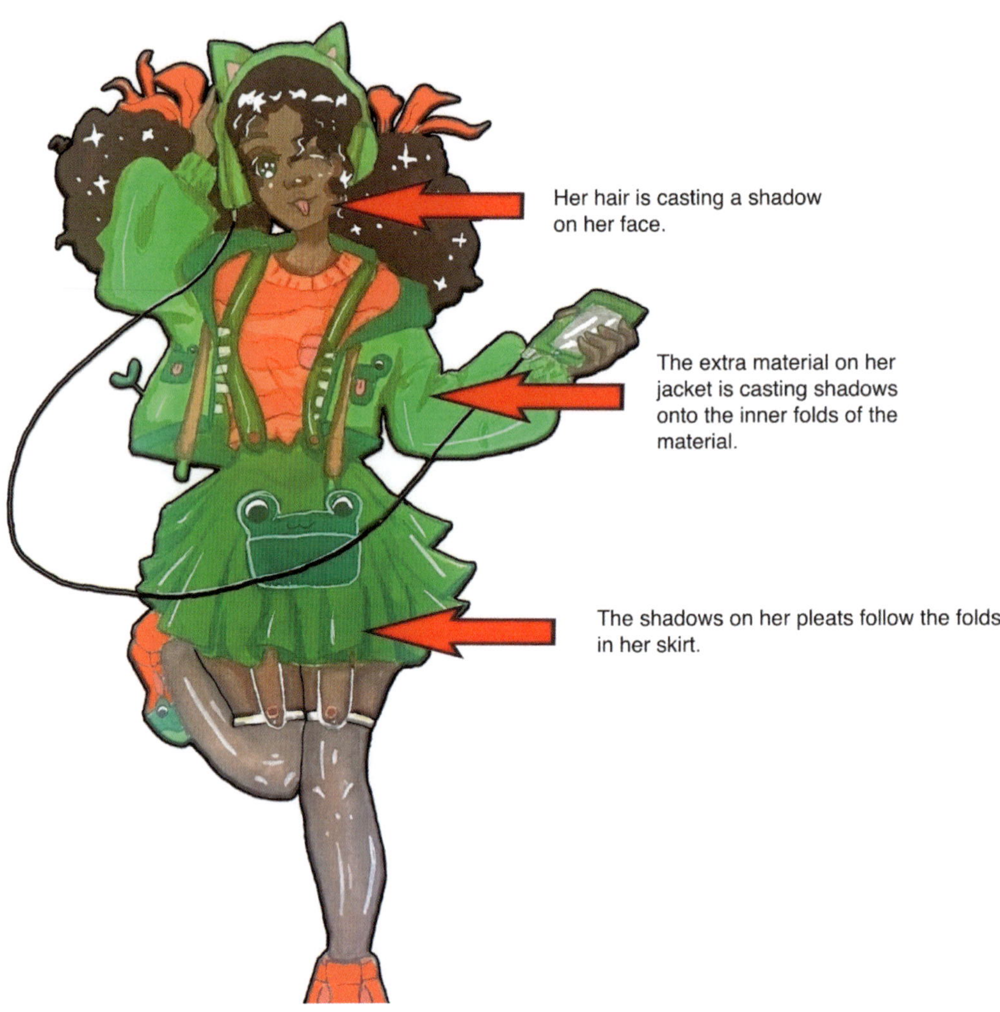

Sketching

A sketch is a simple outlines consisting of minimum strokes, giving an idea of the picture. Sketching is a great way to brainstorm how you may want your final picture to look like.

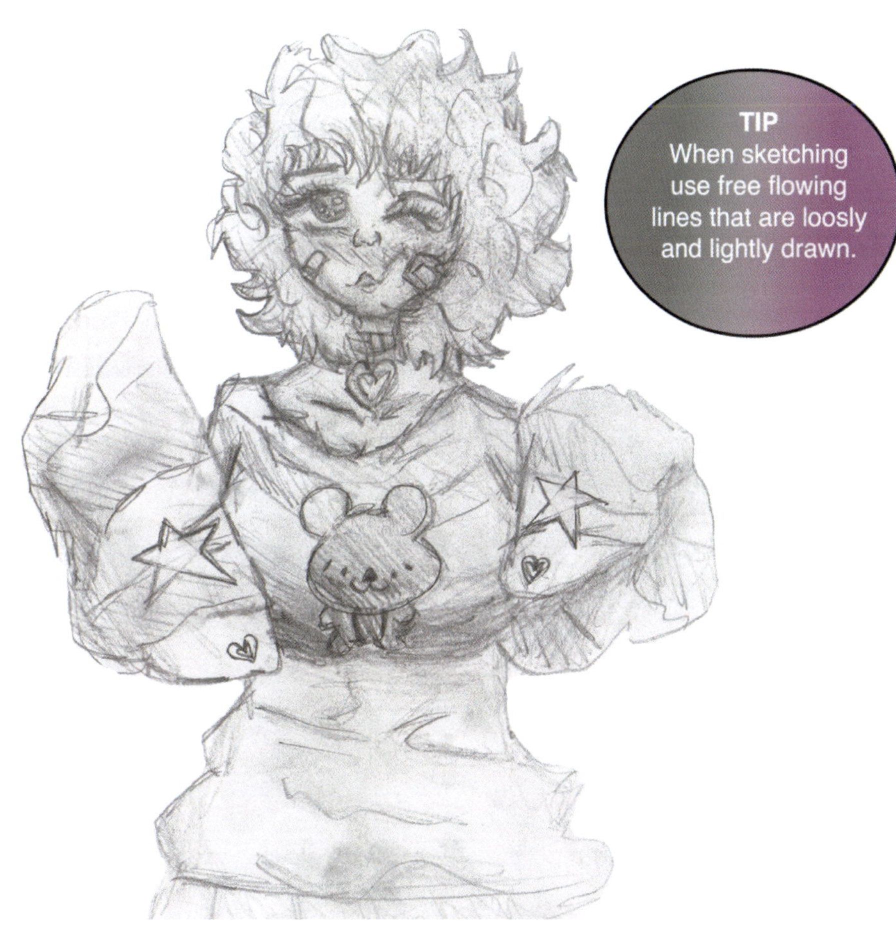

TIP
When sketching use free flowing lines that are loosly and lightly drawn.

Their are 3 main steps to sketching. **Step 1:** sketch loosley and lightly start to create your shape with loose strokes.) **Step 2:** Refine the shape and make your shape a little neater with more solid lines.) **Step 3:** Refine it further by erasing any mistakes and make your lines solid for a final picture.

Step 1: Sketch Loosly	Step 2: Refine Shape	Step 3: Refine it Further

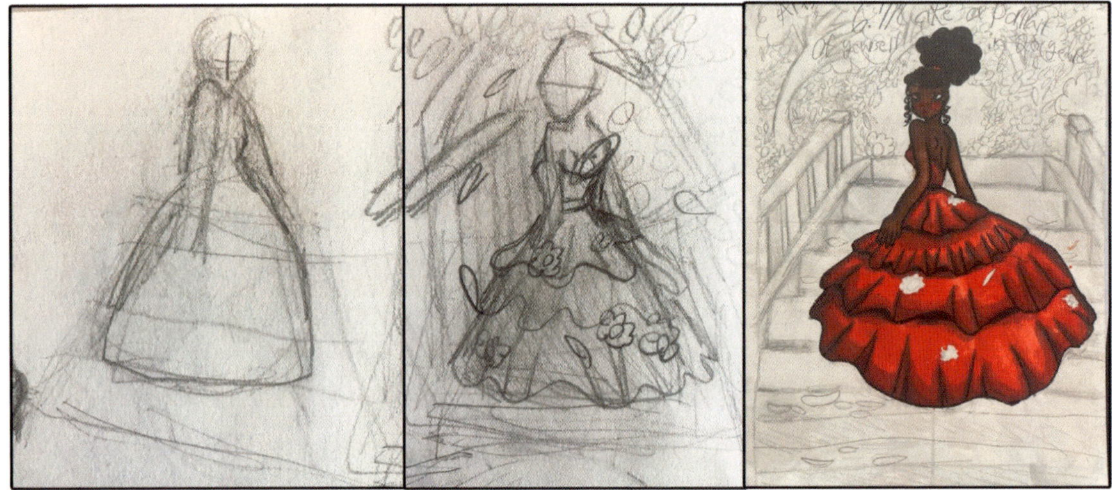

The sketch is a seperate drawing used as a model for the actual drawing. It is a concept. It does not need to be the same as the drawing itself. I like to draw my final drawing on a another sheet of paper seperate from my other sketches.

YOU ARE BEAUTIFUL!!!

Drawing The Anime Head

Let's get started drawing the anime head! In this chapter we will cover how to draw the head, eyes, mouth, nose, and hair. Basicly anything that has to do with the head!

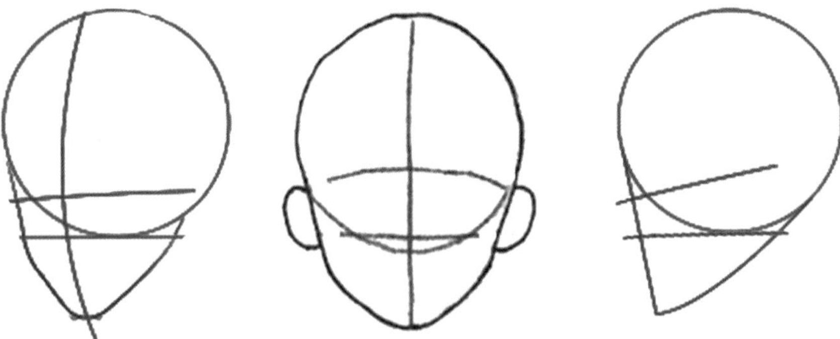

Front Facing Head

Draw a circle and then make a vertical line down the middle. The vertical line will serve as the guide line.The guideline will insure both sides are even. Draw a vertical line on each side of the circle. Make the lines curve inward to make the chin (See step 2). Halfway between the top and bottom of the head draw a horizontal line. Draw another horizontal line just a little bit above the bottom of the circle (See step 3). You will draw the eyes between the two horizontal lines you just created. Use the vertical guideline to place the nose and mouth.

TIP: If you want to make a older person make the lines longer. If you want to make a younger person make the lines shorter.

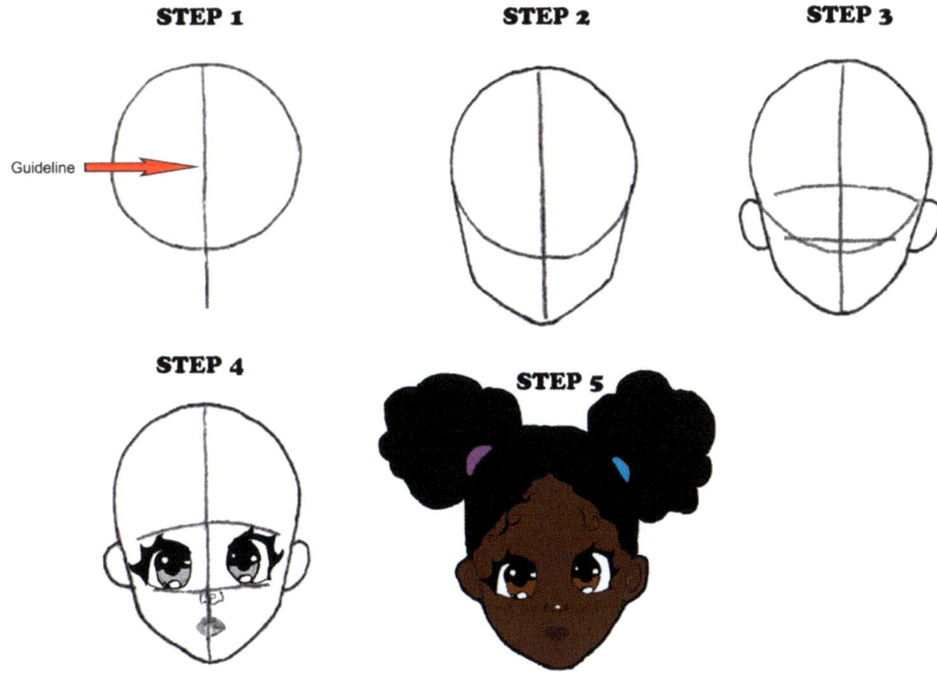

3/4 Facing Head

Draw a circle. Draw the guideline closer to one half of the circle. Then draw a horizontal line (see step 2). Draw a second horizontal line under the bottom of the circle. Draw a vertical line on one side of the circle. Make the line curve inward and back up to the other side of the circle (see step 3). Draw the near eye far away from the center line. Draw the far eye close to the center line. Tip when drawing a boys head extend the tip of his nose past the center line.

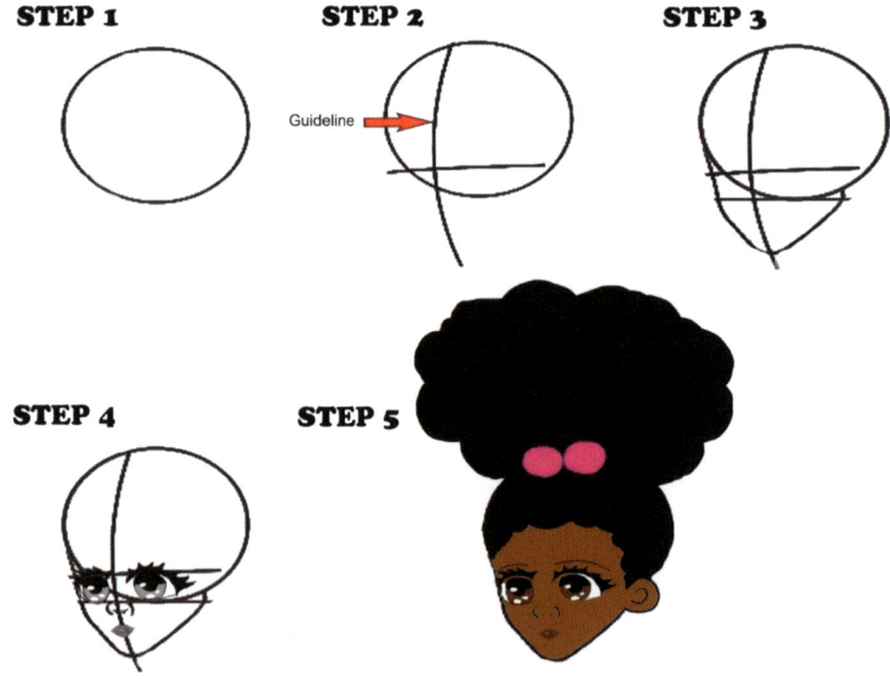

Side Facing Head

Below you will find a simple method for drawing a basic side view of the anime head. Start with drawing a circle. Next draw a horizontal but slightly diagonal line (See step 2). Draw a line vertically in front of the circle like the picture. Then curve the line towards the back of the circle (See step 3). Draw an eye in the center of the guide(See step 4). Next draw the nose and mouth in front of the vertical guide line. Add finishing details (See step 6).

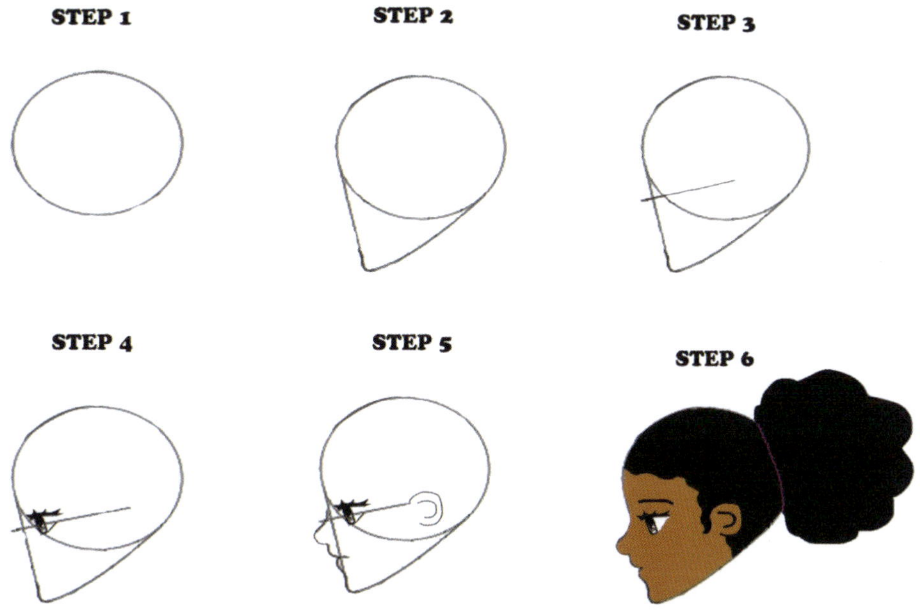

How to Draw Anime Boy Head

Anime boys faces are not as round as anime girls. Their faces are more narrower. Their jaw line is slightly longer. The neck on an anime boy is drawn closer to the Jawline to give him a more muscular look. The eyes are more narrow or slanted.

TIP: The more slanted you make the eyes the older the character will look.

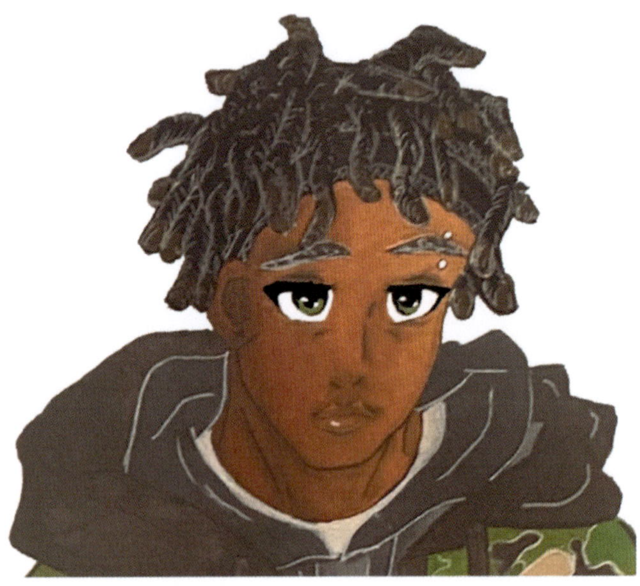

The Difference Between Anime Girl and Boy Face

Girl	Boy
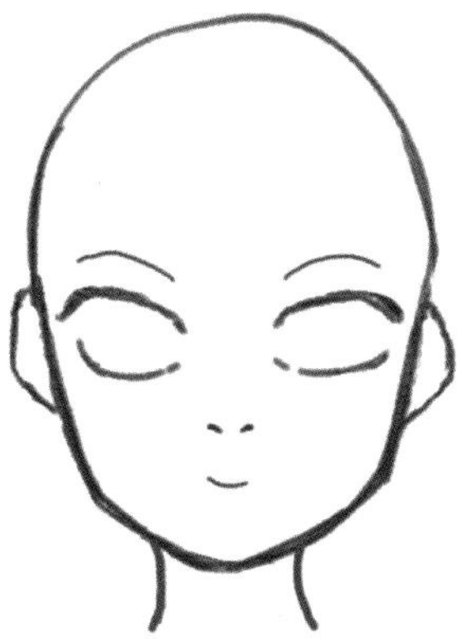	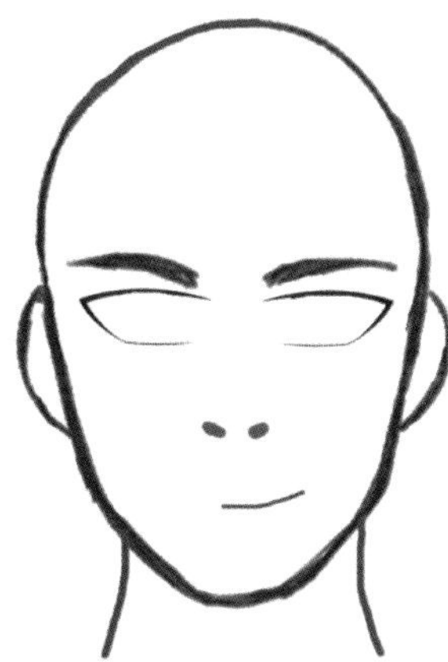
Rounder Face	Longer Face
Rounder Eyes	Smaller slanted Eyes
Slimmer Neck	Thicker Neck

How to Draw an Anime Boy Head Step by Step

To make an anime boy face Draw a egg shape circle. Make a vertical line down the middle. Make the vertical line longer than the circle. This will insure both sides are even. Create a guideline for the eyes by drawing a horizontal line 1/3 from the bottom of the circle. Draw another horizontal line under the guideline near the bottom of the circle. The eyes will go between the two lines. To draw the chin and jaw draw two sets of lines down from the circle. Make the jaw line slightly longer for a boy. Make sure you use angled lines to connect your jaw lines to form your chin. When drawing the neck draw the sides of the neck closer to the jawline. When drawing a boys eyes make them more narrow or slated.

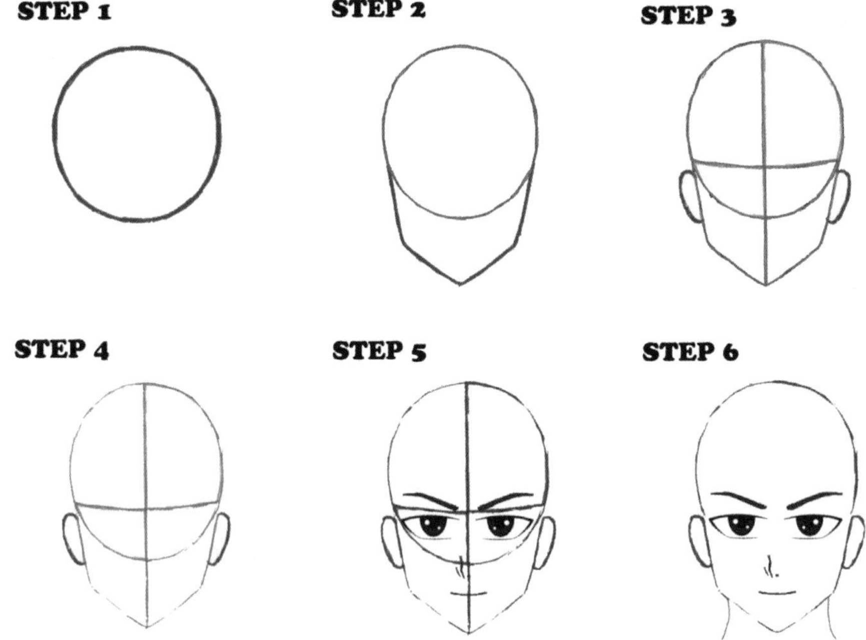

YOU ARE POWERFUL!!!

How to Draw Shiny Eyes

Now that you've learned how to draw an anime head, let's move on to drawing the eyes!

Anime eyes are iconic! The most popular anime eyes are usually doe-eyed and capture lots of light! However anime eyes come in many different sizes from super big to slanted more realistic eyes. You can use any colors in your anime eyes to make them unique.

TIP: When coloring your anime use your white gel pen to create the light in the eyes. It will make your anime's eyes pop!

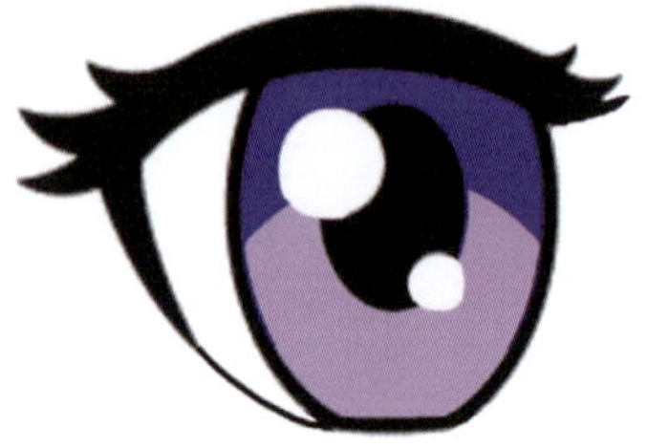

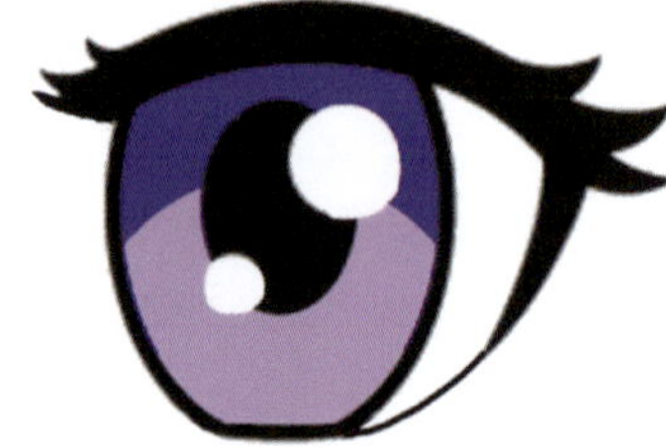

Highlights in the eyes are what makes them appear shiny. Highlights are created by making two white circles in the eye. One circle is larger than the other. If you want to add even more shine to the eyes create more white circles. I have used up to five in some of my drawings.

How to Draw Anime Girl Eyes Step by Step

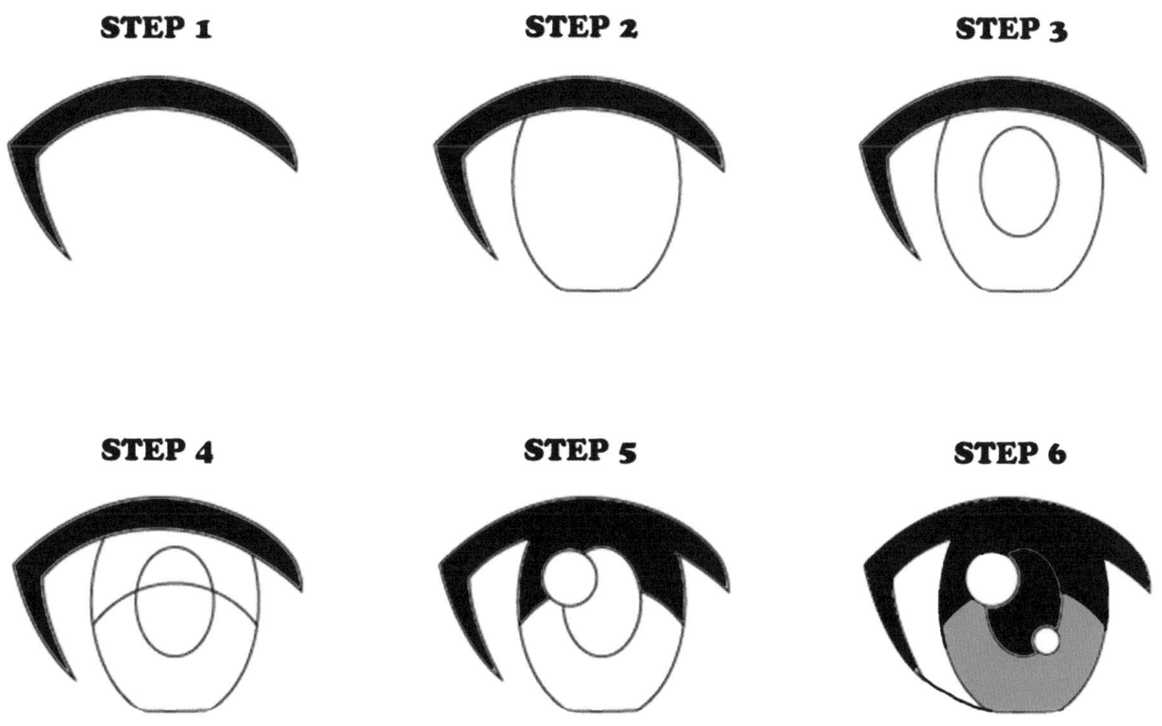

Anime Boy Eyes

Anime boy eyes are slightly different than girl eyes. Boy eyes have a more narrow shape. For the iris we will use a semi circle instead of a oval. We will create shine in the males eye by making two small white circles in the middle of the iris.

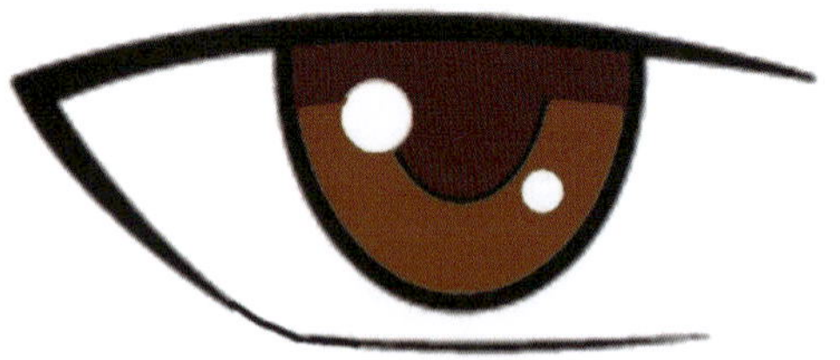

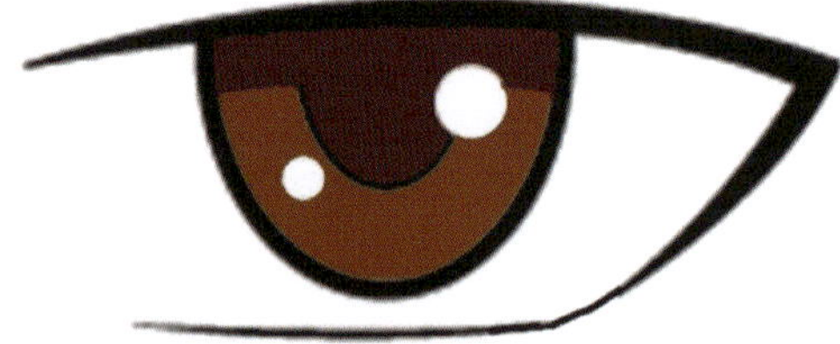

How to Draw Anime Boy Eyes Step by Step

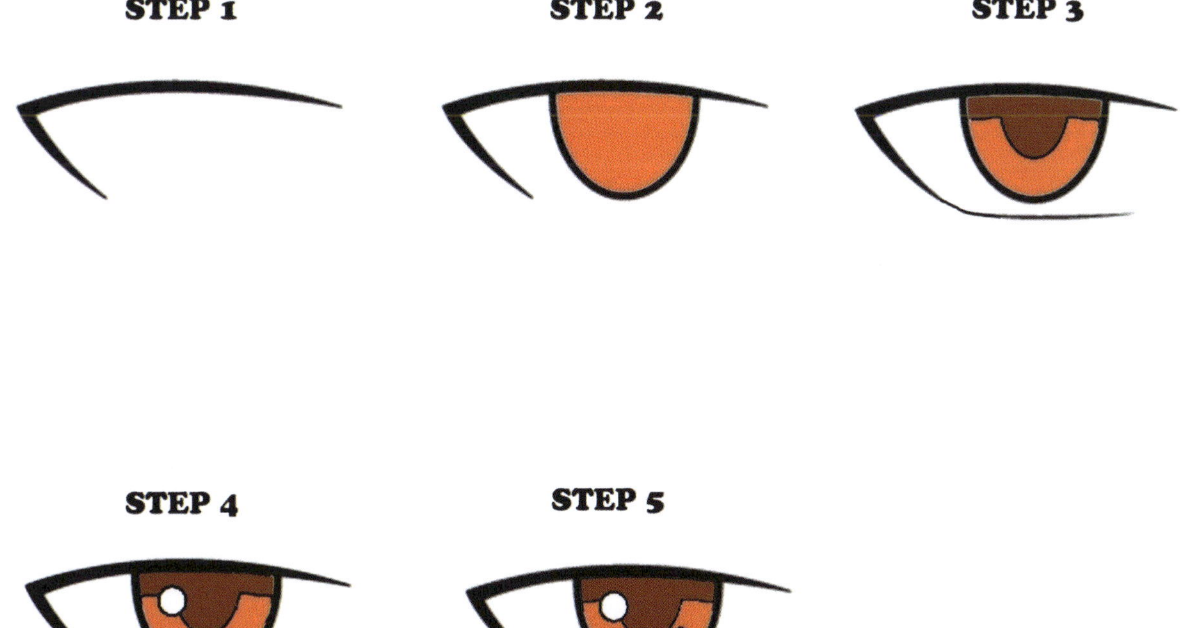

Drawing Facial Features

Anime characters typically have small facial features. However this is a book about how to draw black anime. So I'm going to show you some ways to make your characters look black and not just simply a white anime colored brown. Black people have so many different features that are all beautiful and unique. Black noses and mouthes come in a variety of shapes and sizes. Lets get started with learning how to draw a black anime nose.

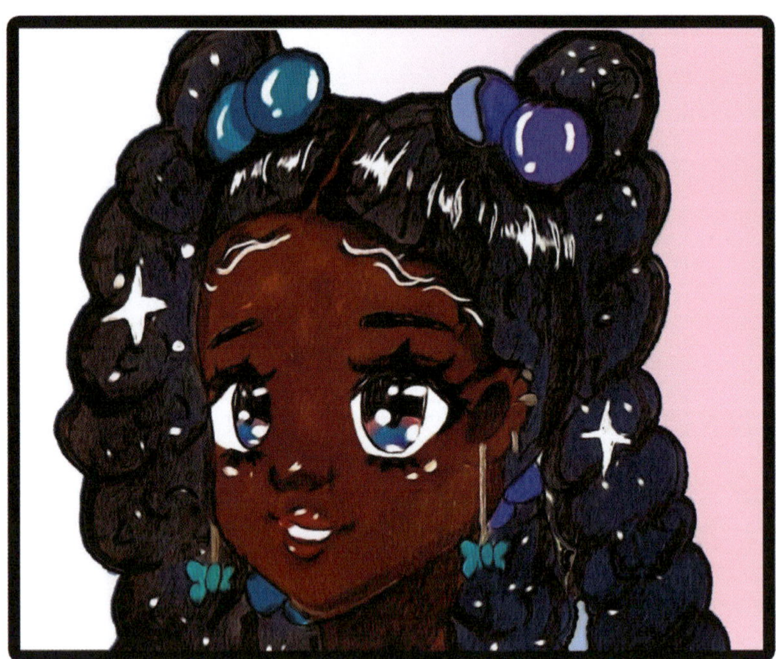

The Anime Nose

The typical anime are drawn with simple noses. Most of the time you will simply see a line, two small dots or even nothing at all. However I find that when I draw my black characters with these types of noses the characters usually doesn't look black in the final drawing. They usually turn out looking white with black skin. To draw a black character I like to draw slightly pudgy noses to give my characters a more ethnic look. look at the pictures below. These are my favorite noses to use for my black characters.

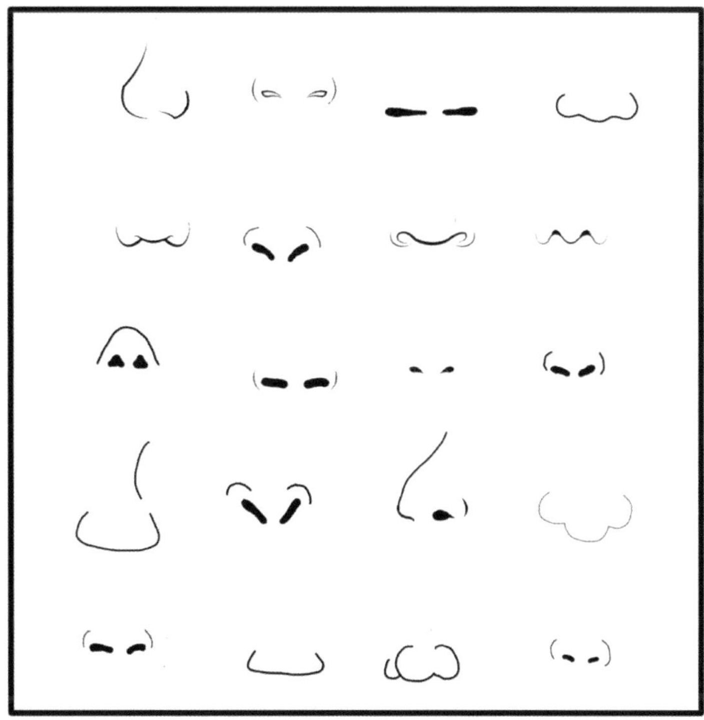

The Anime Mouth

The anime mouth can range from as simple as a single line to more complex for expressions. To draw black anime mouths I like to make the lips a little fuller than the typical anime. I accomplish this with shading. Below I have drawn some of my favorite lips for my black anime characters.

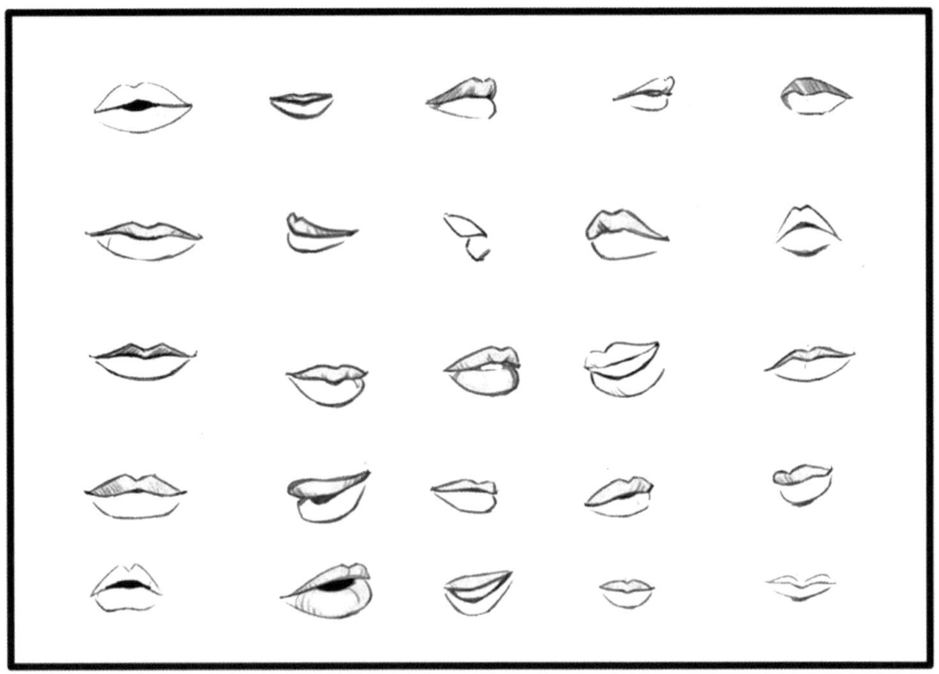

How to Create Shine on the Mouth

Creating shine on the mouth is anouther way to make the lips appear fuller. First you have to draw lips and shade them. Then take your white gel pen and make two white dots on the top lip and one on the bottom, or one dot on the top lip and two on the bottom. Two dots on each lip is the max I would add shine. Of corse if you want less shine only add one white dot on each lip. How much shine you add is completely up to you. Be creative!

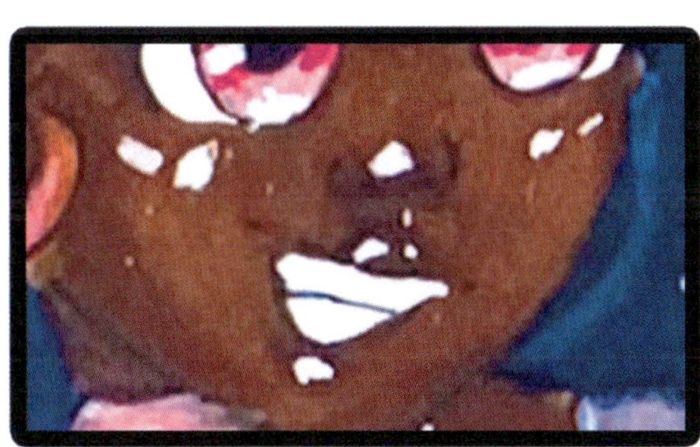

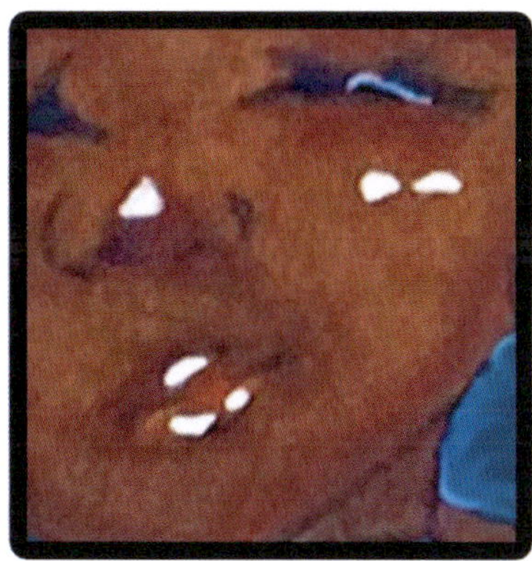

YOU DESCEND FROM GREATNESS!!!

How to Draw Natural Afro Textured Hairstyles (Locs, Twist, Braids, and Fades)

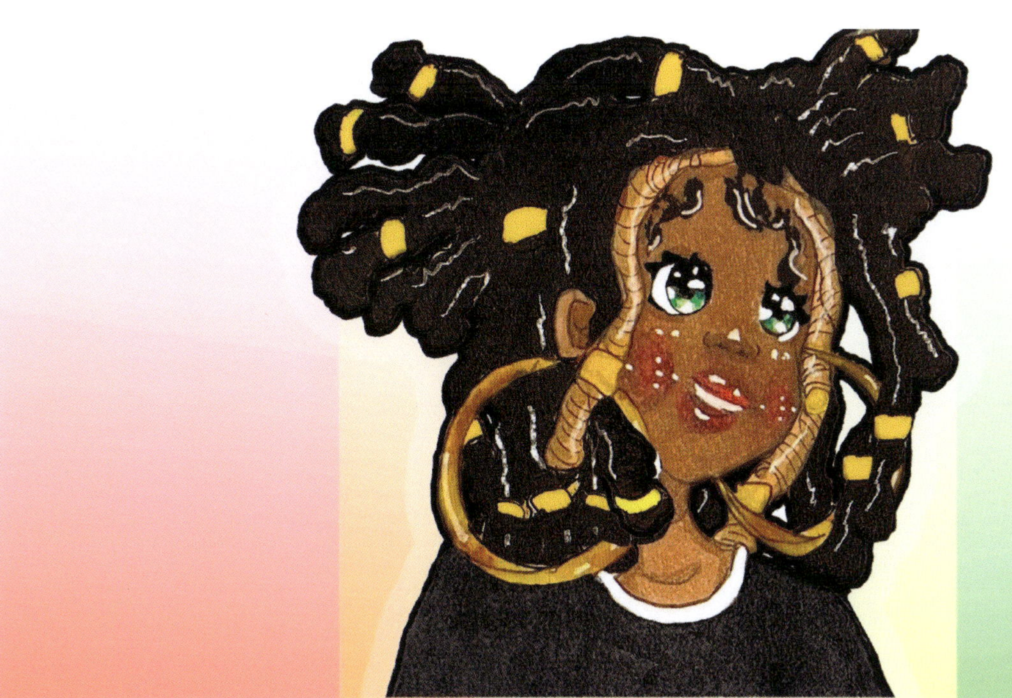

How to Draw Natural Afro Textured Hairstyles (Locs, Twist, Braids, and Fades)

In this chapter I will teach you how to draw natural black hairstyles. Black people have different hair types but most of my black anime have type 3A - 4C hair so we will be focusing more on those hair types for the hairstyles you will learn. This system for classifying hair comes from Andre Walkers hair typing system. If your going to draw black hair it's good to formalize yourself with the different hair types. Below is a picture for you to view the different hair types and patterns.

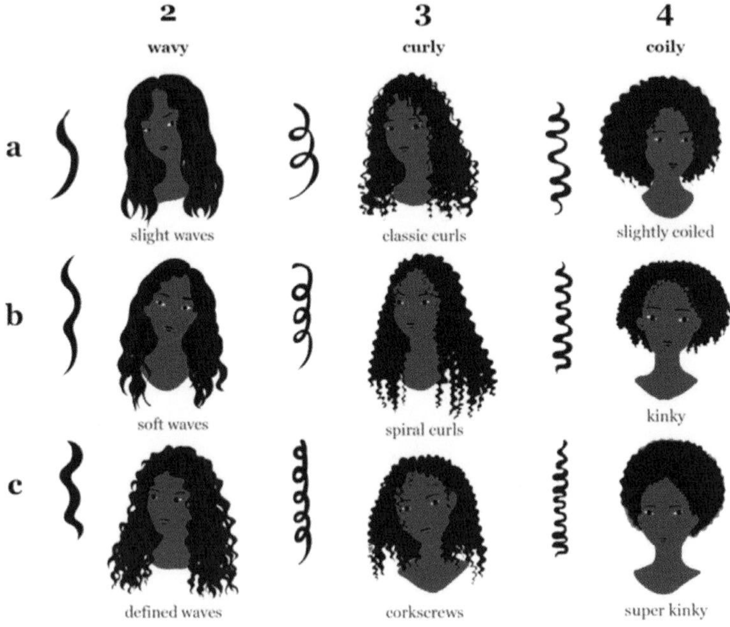

Afro

Most people try to portray afro textured hair as a perfect circle but that's just not the case. to properly draw this type of hair you need to draw a lot of contours. Follow the steps below to learn how to create a textured afro.

Remember practice makes perfect!

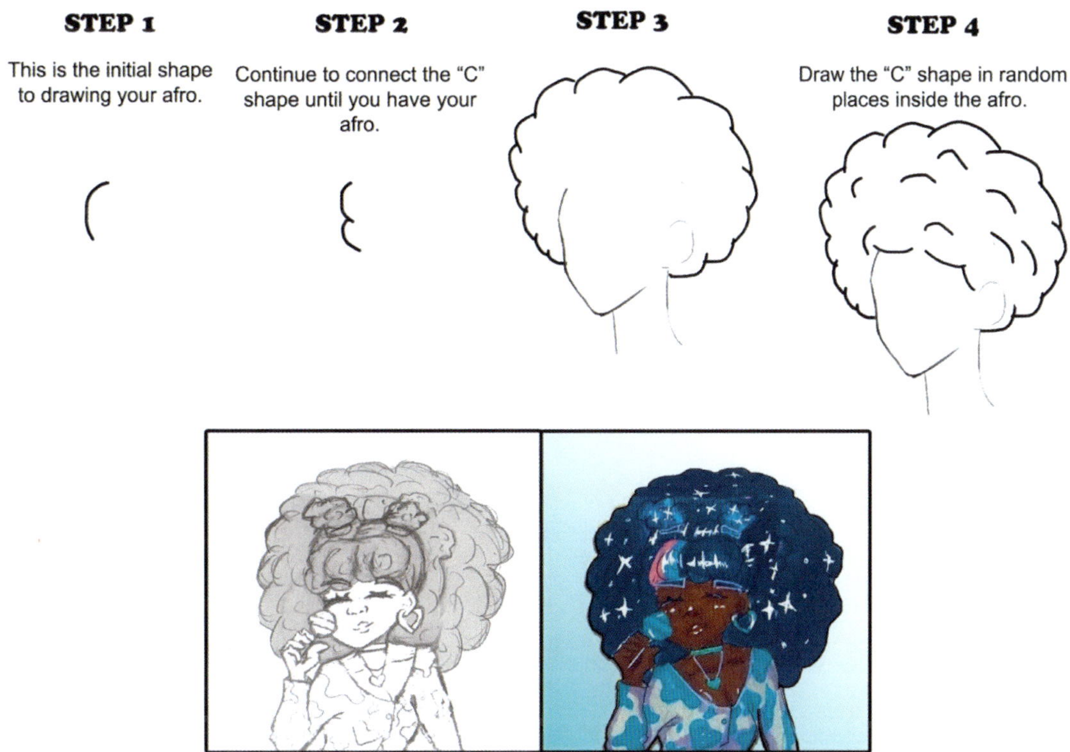

Braids

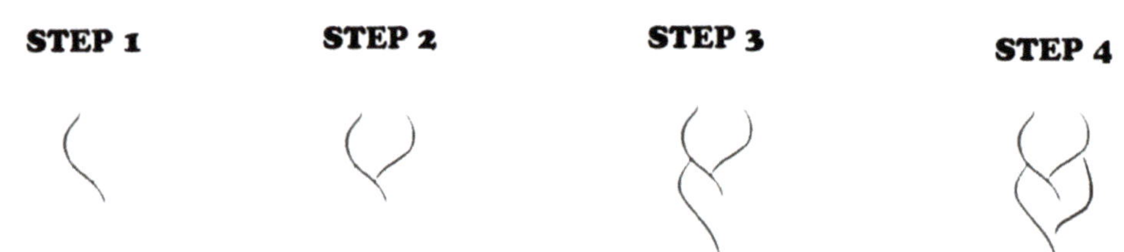

STEP 5

Add more braids until you achieve your desired style

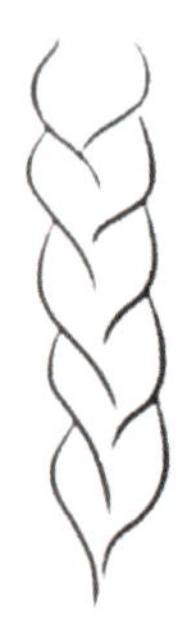

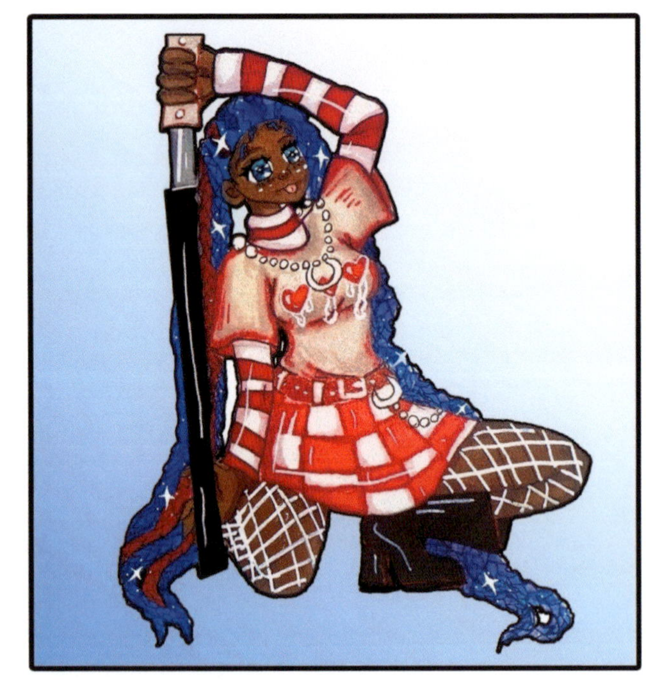

Twist

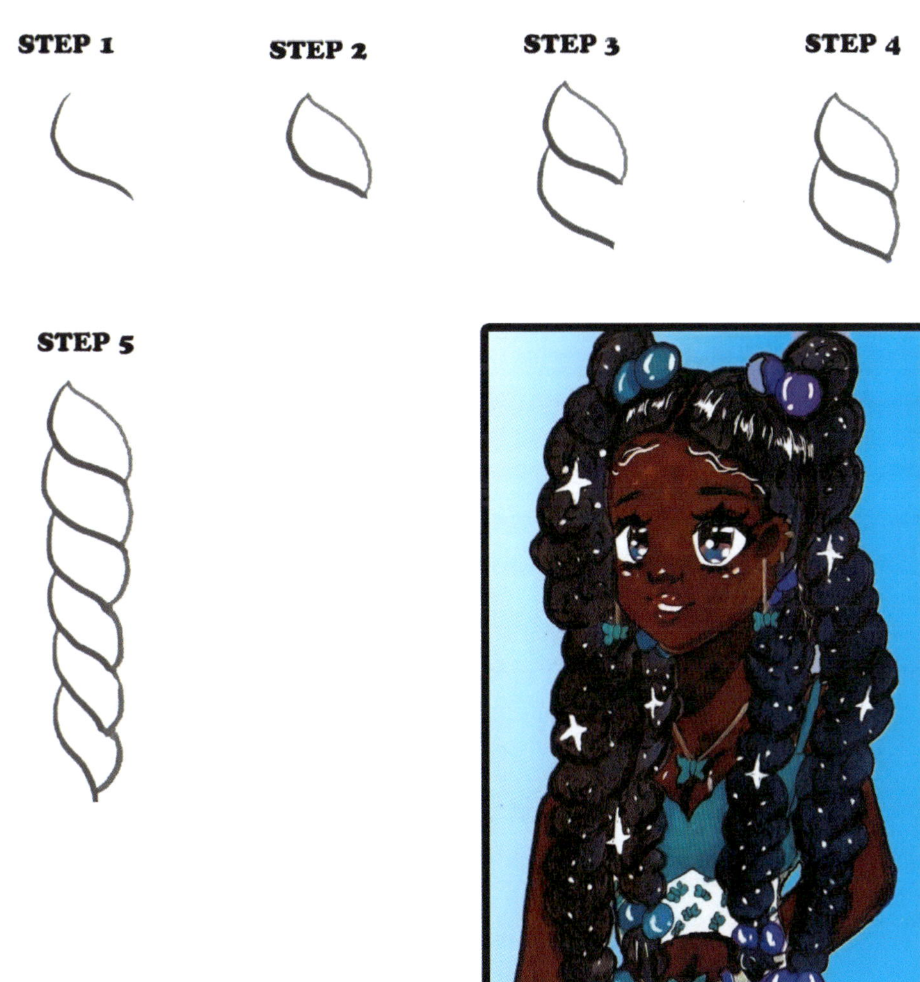

Locs

STEP 1

Draw the shape of your loc

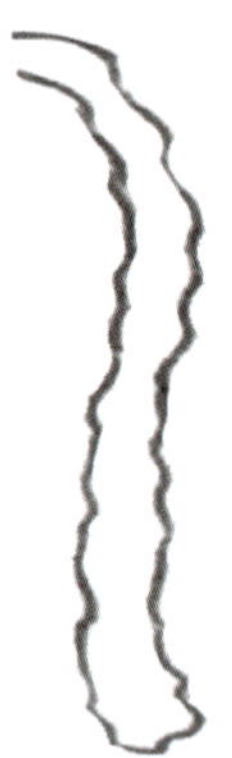

STEP 2

Now is the time to practice contouring. Make a slight C shape like the picture below inside your loc. Doing this will make your loc start to look more rounded. Continue making that shape all the way up the loc.

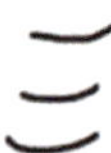

STEP 3

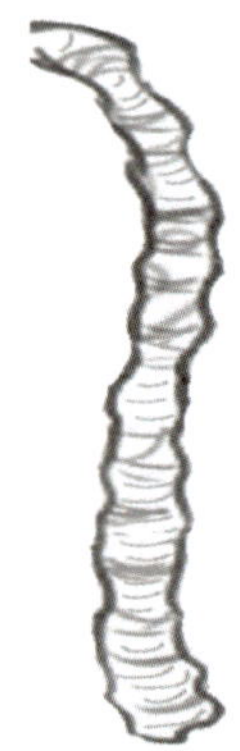

STEP 4

Add as many locs as you want

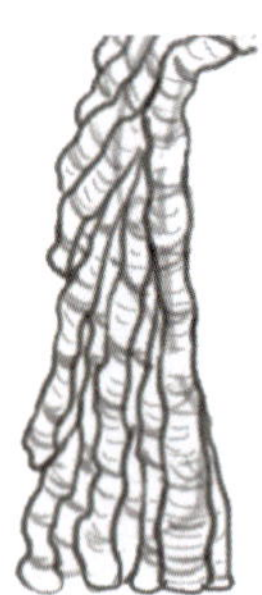

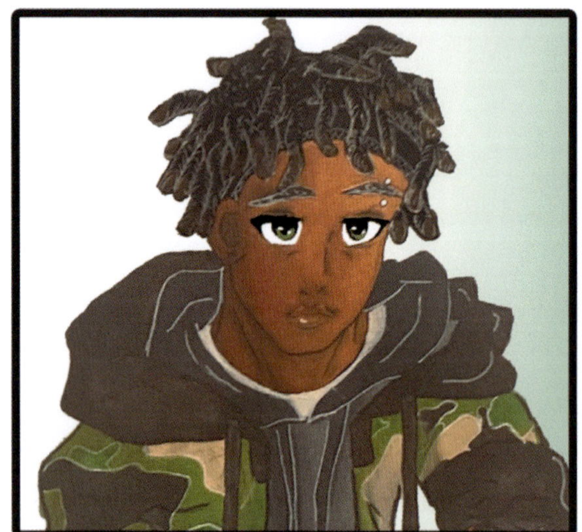

Fade Haircut

STEP 1

STEP 2

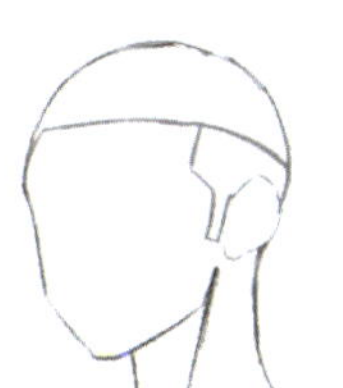

STEP 3

Use the hatching shading technique to achieve the fade. The fade should be darkest near the top of the head and gradually get lighter.

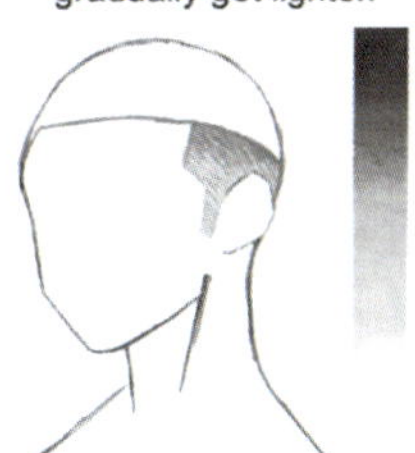

STEP 4

Continue with this step if you want your anime to have just a short cut fade with no long hair at the top. If you want your anime to have longer hair at the top **SKIP TO STEP 5**. For short cut just color the to part of the head in with a darker color than you used to make the initial hatching fade.

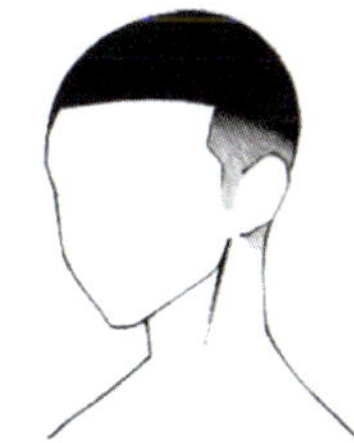

STEP 5

If you want your anime to have a little more hair at the top of his head start making the "C" shape like you learned in the How to make a Afro section. Continue making the shape until you have your desired level of hair at the top of the head.

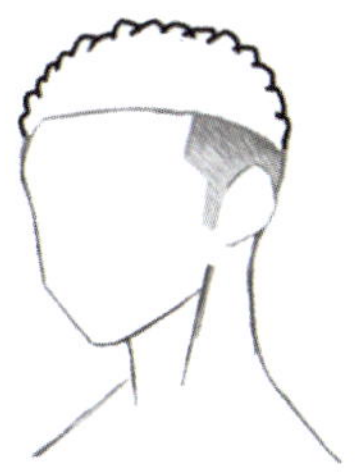

STEP 6

Randomly place the "C" shape around the inside of the hair.

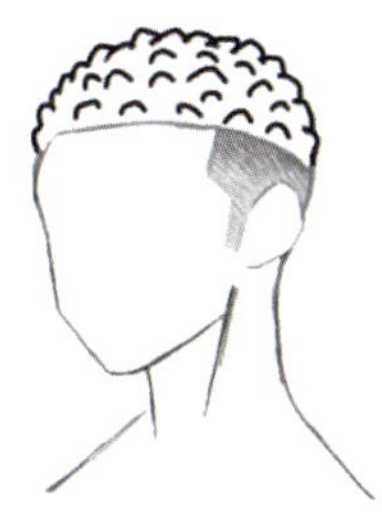

STEP 7

If you want your anime to have a design in his head take your eraser and erase part of the hatching fade until you get the design you want. in the pic below I simply wanted stripes for his hair design.

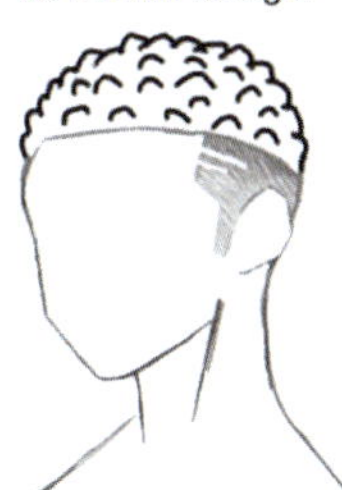

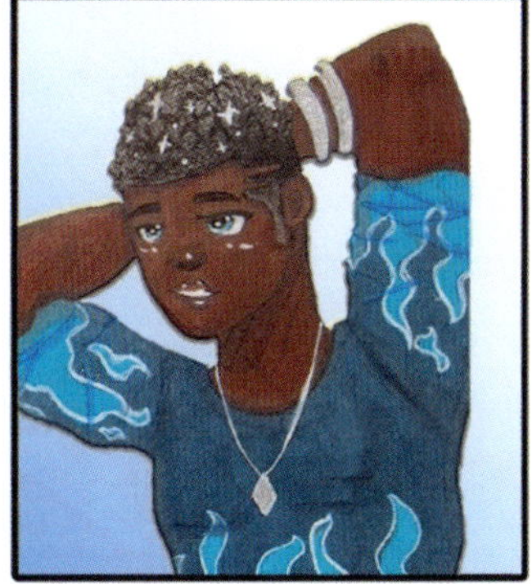

TIP: If you want your anime to have black hair you will be able to see the texture you create by using you white gel pen to highlight it.

Fade Hairstyles

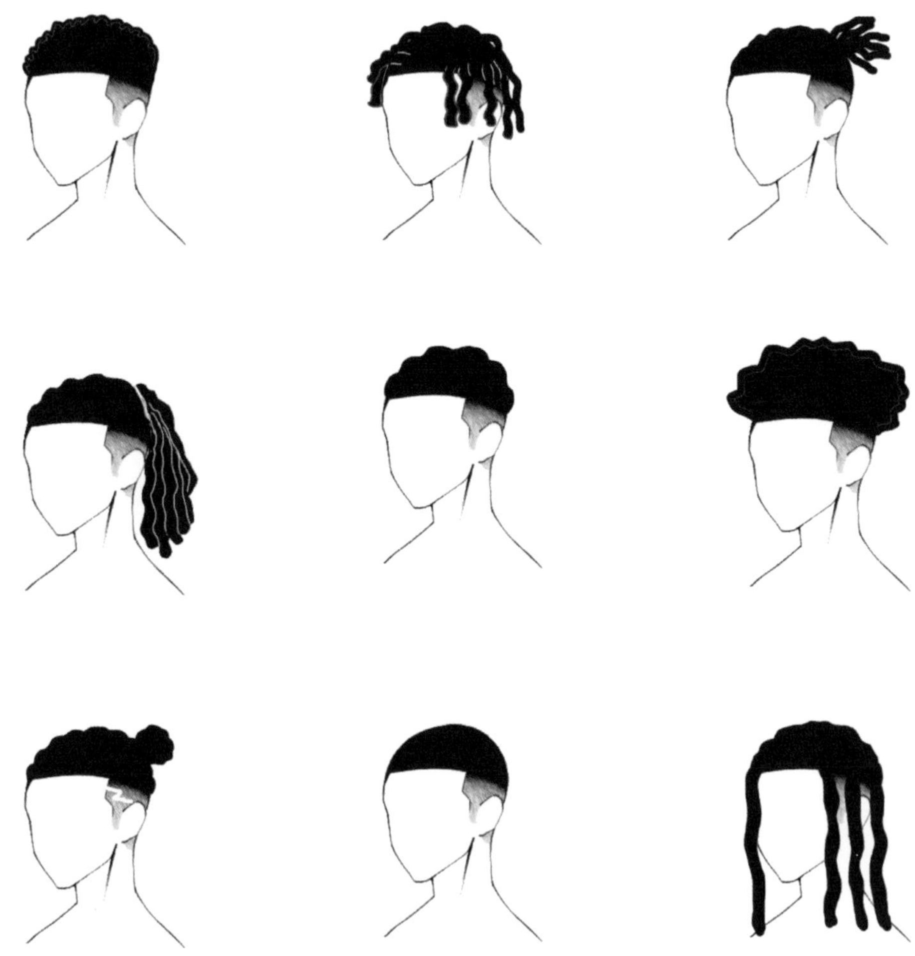

Afro Hairstyles

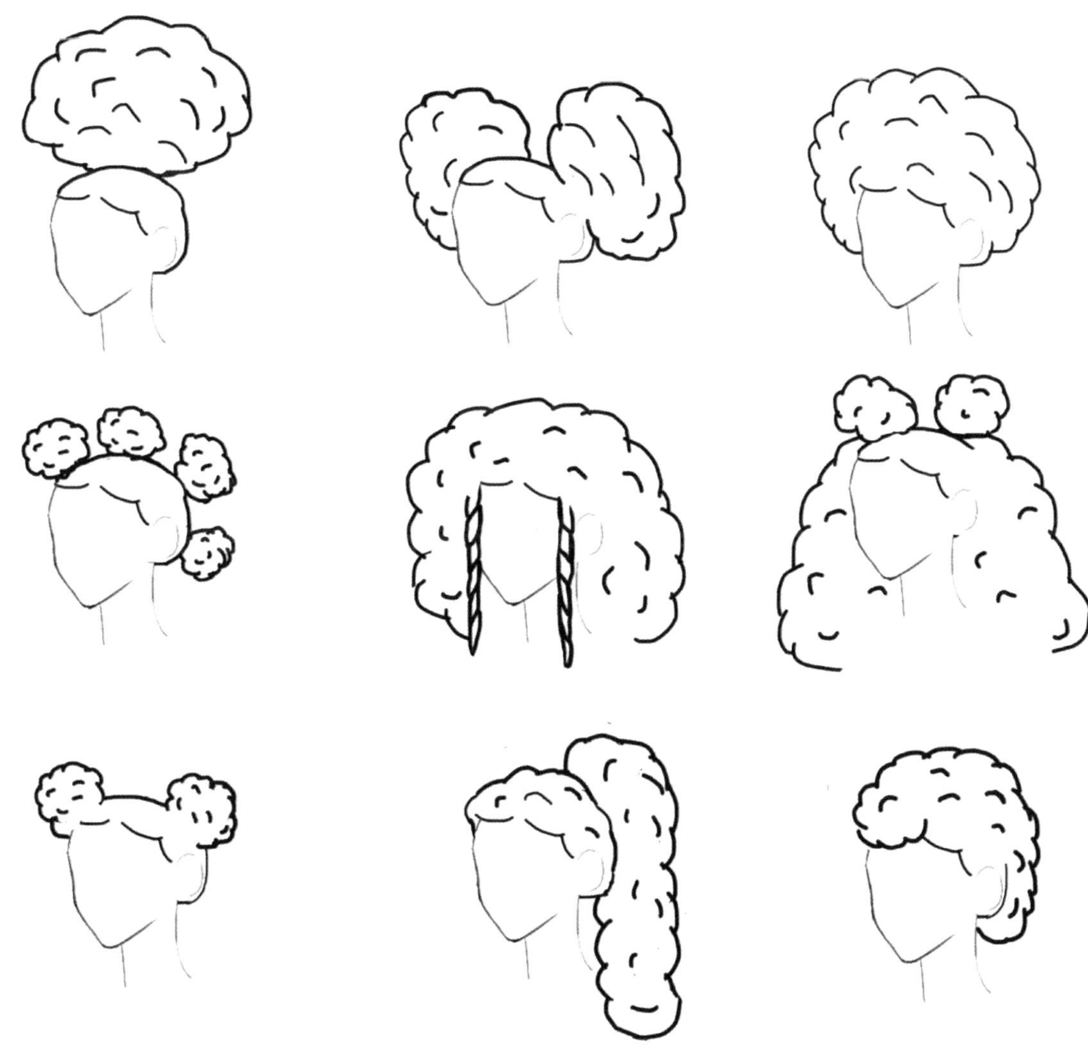

How I Create Shine on Afro Textured Hair

To create shine on afro textured hair you will need your white gel pen. This step is the last step after you have finished shading or coloring the hair. Take your white gel pen and randomly place dots and stars in the hair. For the parts of the hair that are straight Draw a group of connected random white lines in the hair with your white gel pen. The lines should go in the direction the hair is going.

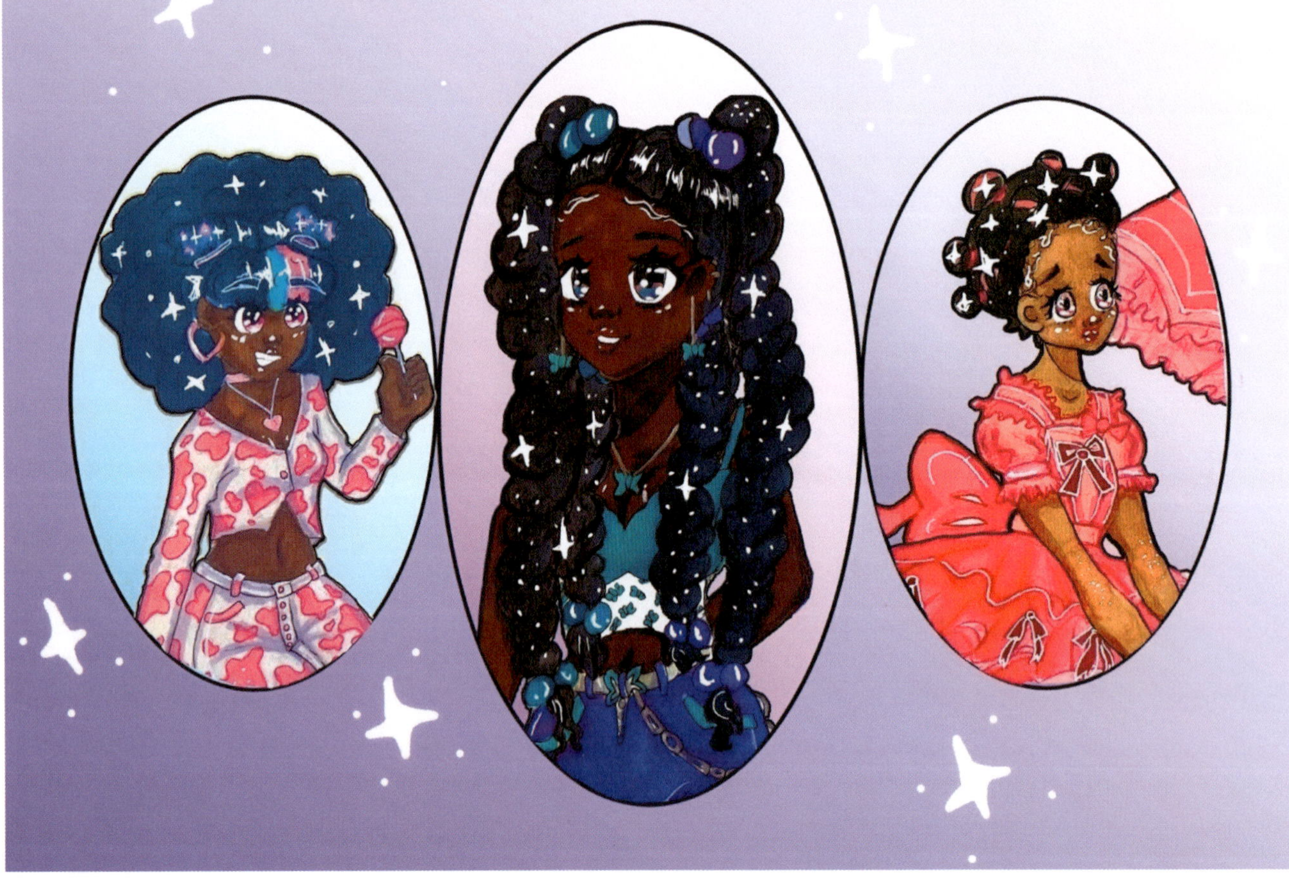

YOU ARE FEARLESS!!!

Anime Body

The anime body is one of the most important parts to drawing your anime! In this chapter I will teach you the correct proportions to draw your anime. Let's get started!

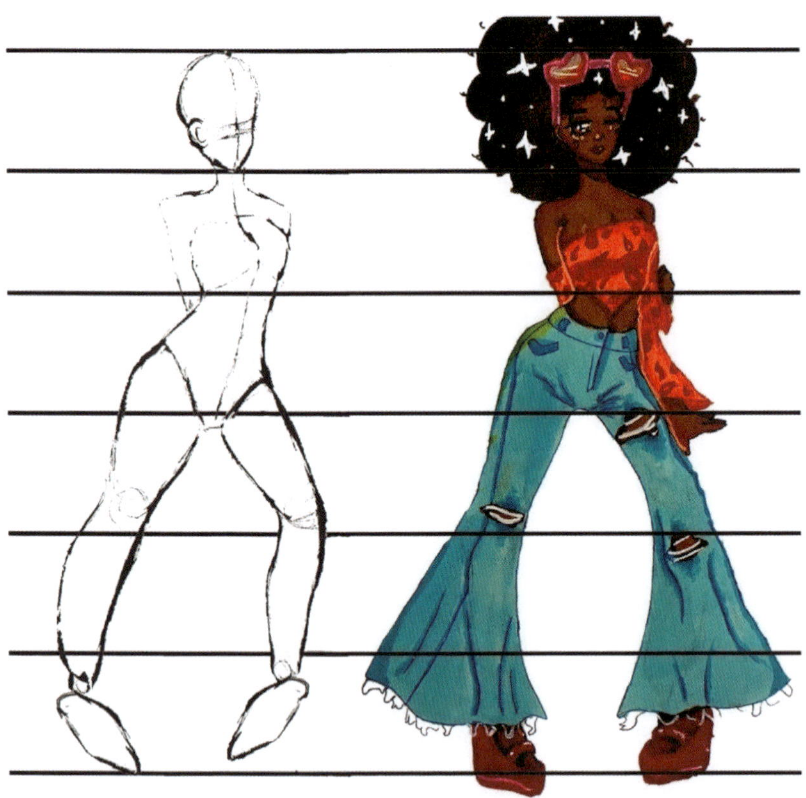

Body Proportions

Making a proportion grid is a great way to measure out your characters body proportions. Use the length of the head as a measurement unit like shown in the picture below. Make a horizontal line at the top and bottom of the head. Each section of the body will be roughly the same size of the head.

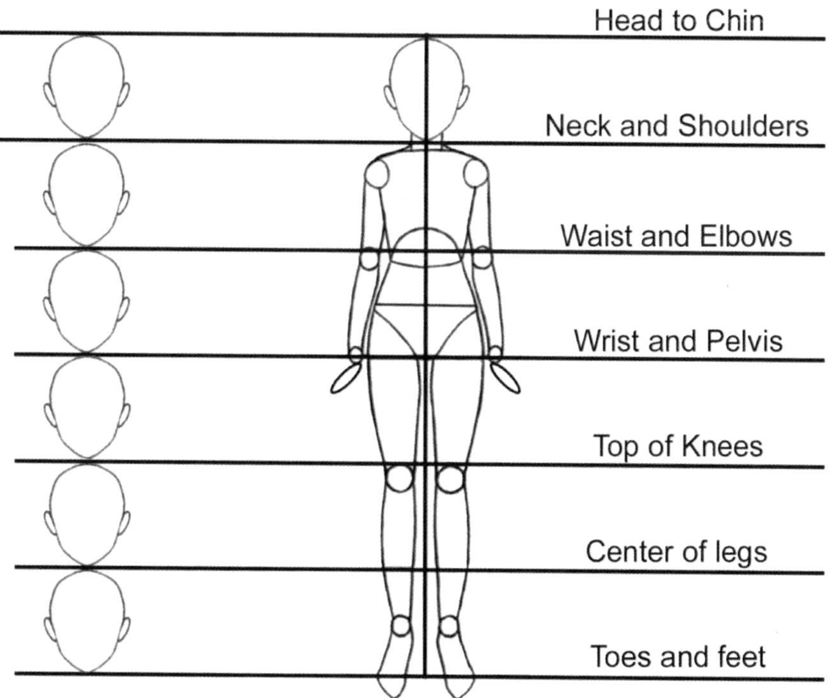

You can learn to draw anime bodies without lines by starting off with STEP 1 as shown below. Starting off with this step will help you gauge the proportions of your character. In STEP 2 you will notice I use shapes to make the character. You make certain shapes a little wider if you want a more shaply character. Using the basic shapes should really help you form your character. STEP 3 you form these basic shapes into your animes final form. STEP 4 all that's left to do is color and shade.

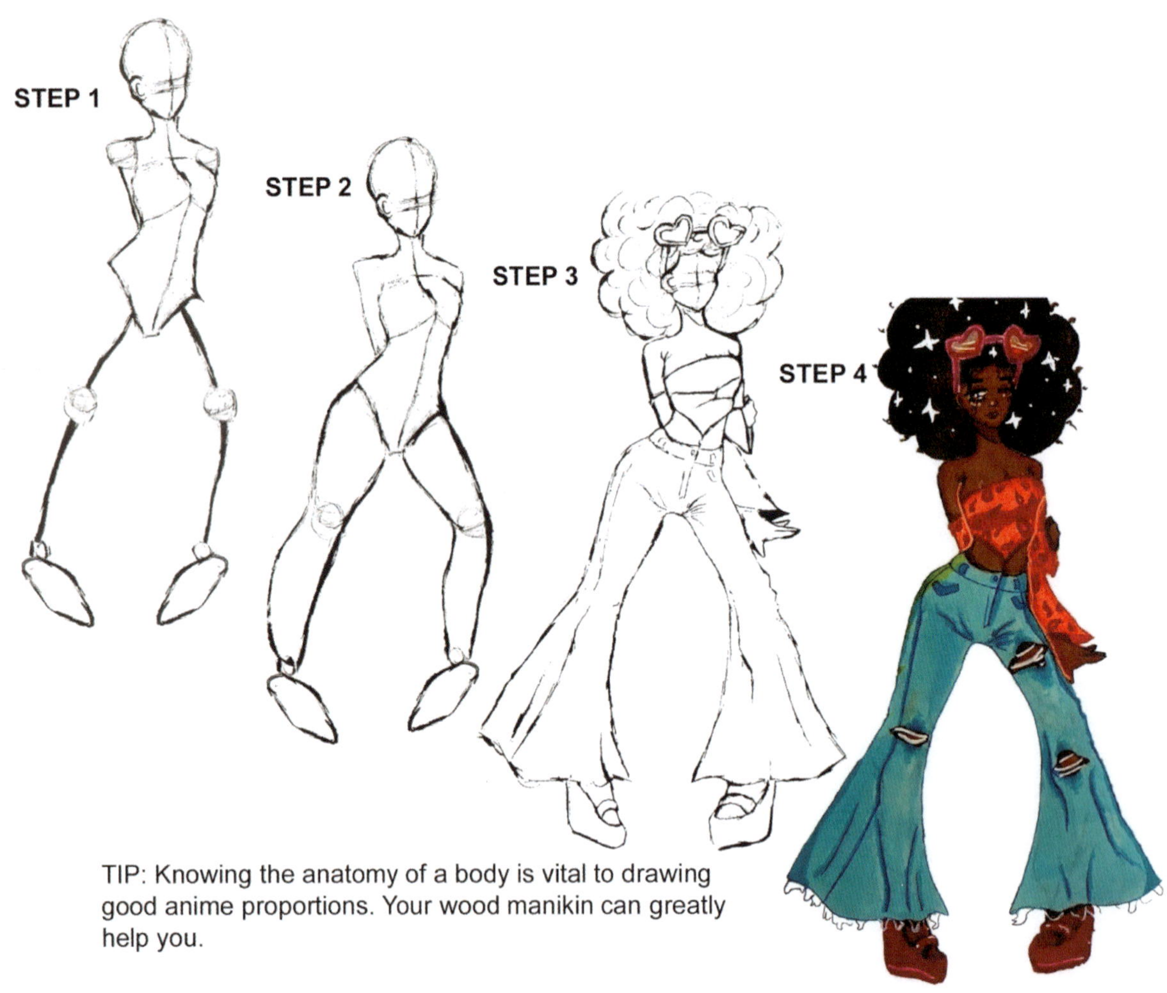

TIP: Knowing the anatomy of a body is vital to drawing good anime proportions. Your wood manikin can greatly help you.

Drawing the Anime Hands

In this chapter you will be learning how to draw anime hands. Anime hands are hard to draw, so I will be showing you a simple method using shapes! Lets get started!

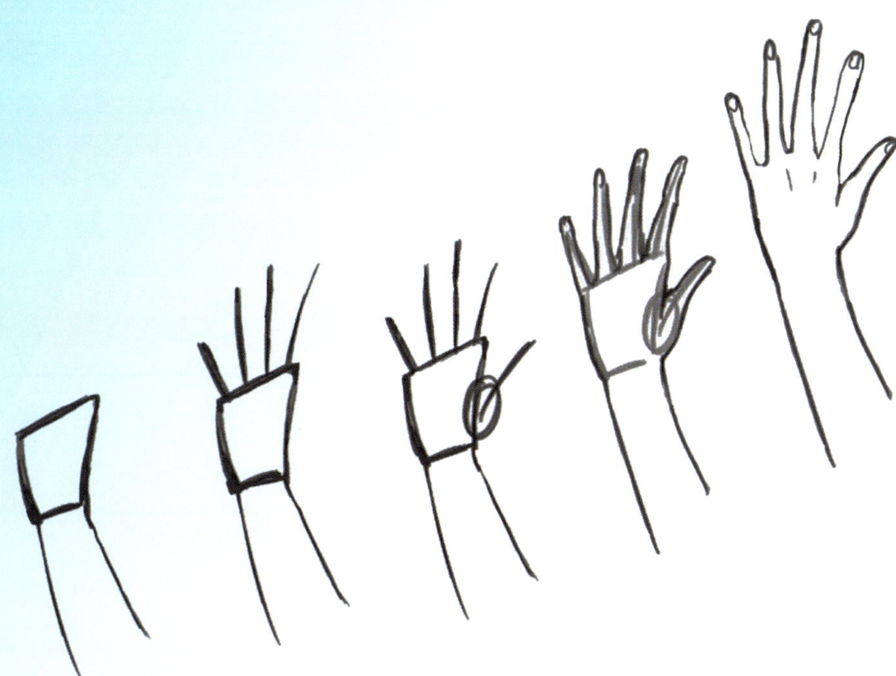

Drawing the Anime hand step by step

Now that you've learned to draw the anime body it's time to learn to draw the hands The easiest way to learn to draw hands is by using shapes. Follow the step by step pictures below to help you learn to draw the perfect anime hands.
Remember practice makes perfect!

STEP 1 **STEP 2** 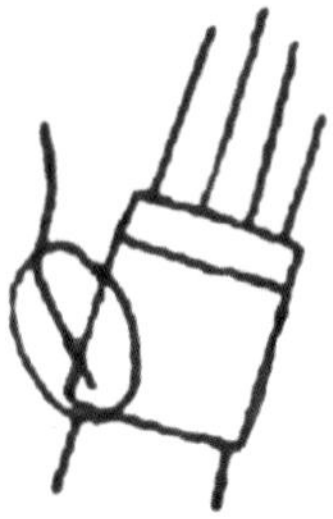 **STEP 3** 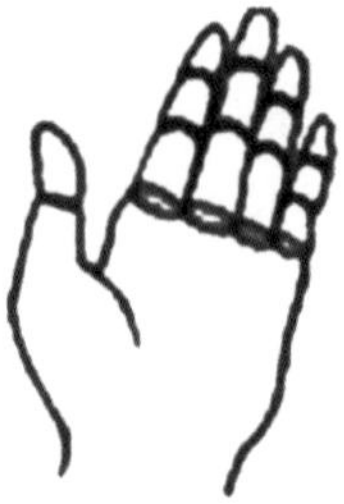 **STEP 4**

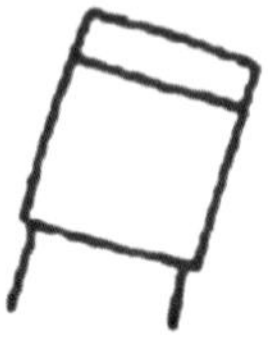

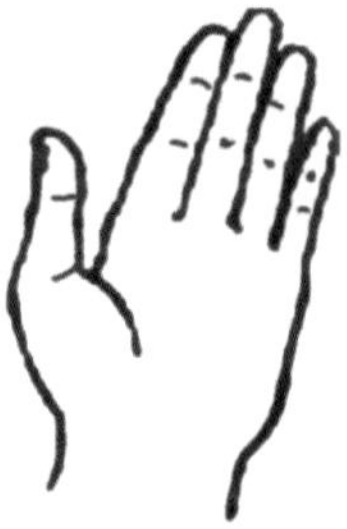

Drawing the Anime hand step by step

Using shapes you will be able to create a peace sign. Follow the steps below to learn how. Remember practice makes perfect!

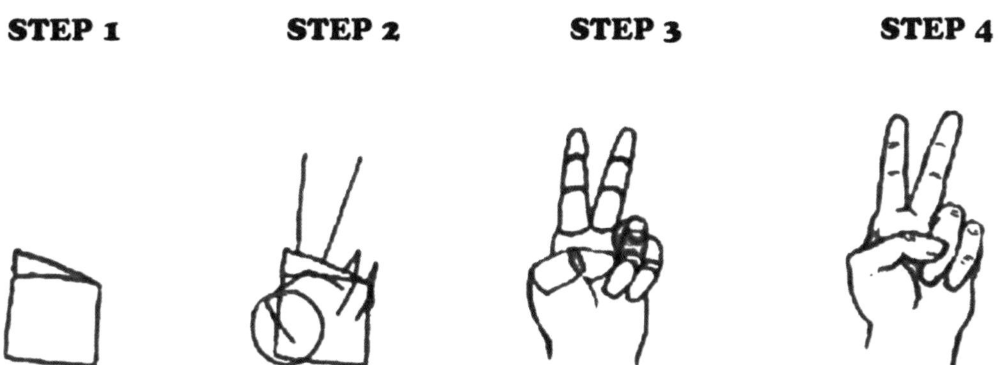

Drawing the Anime Feet

Now that you've learned to draw the anime hands it's time to learn to draw the feet. Just like drawing the anime hands the feet can also be made by using various shapes. In this chapter I will give you step by step instruction on the easiest way to make feet. Let's get started!

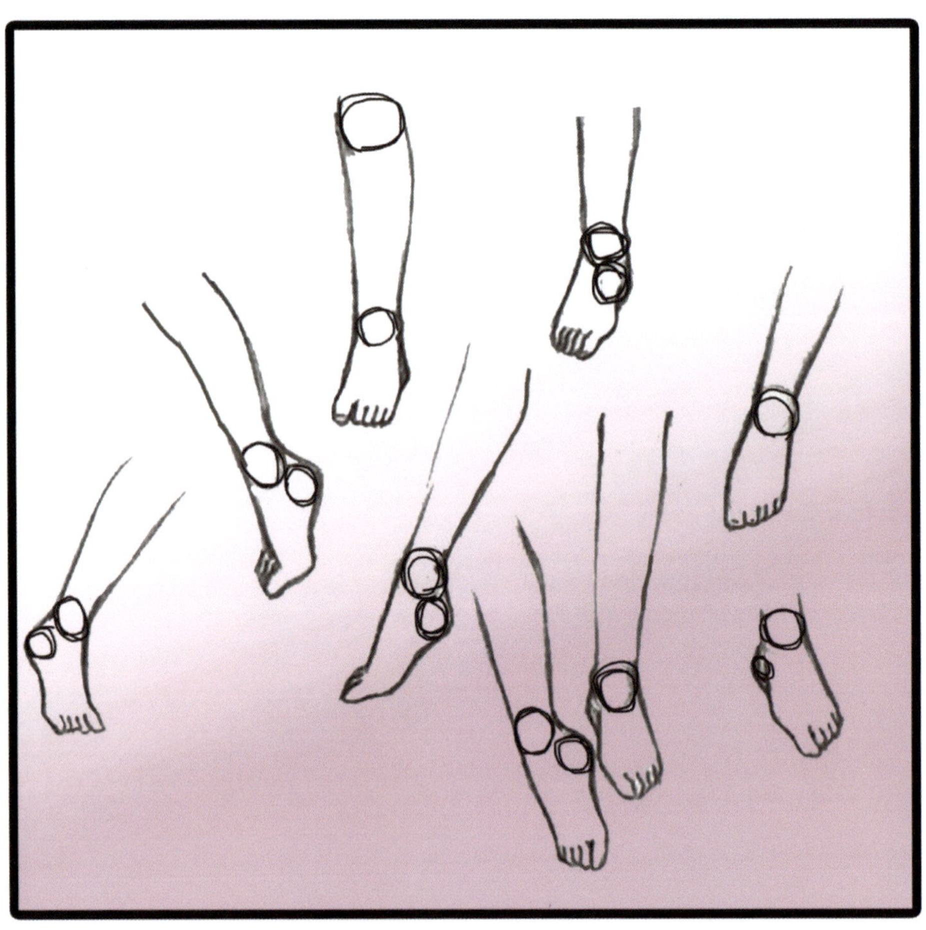

Front of Foot

Below you can see how I used shapes to make the front of the anime foot.
Follow the steps below to learn to draw the front of the foot.

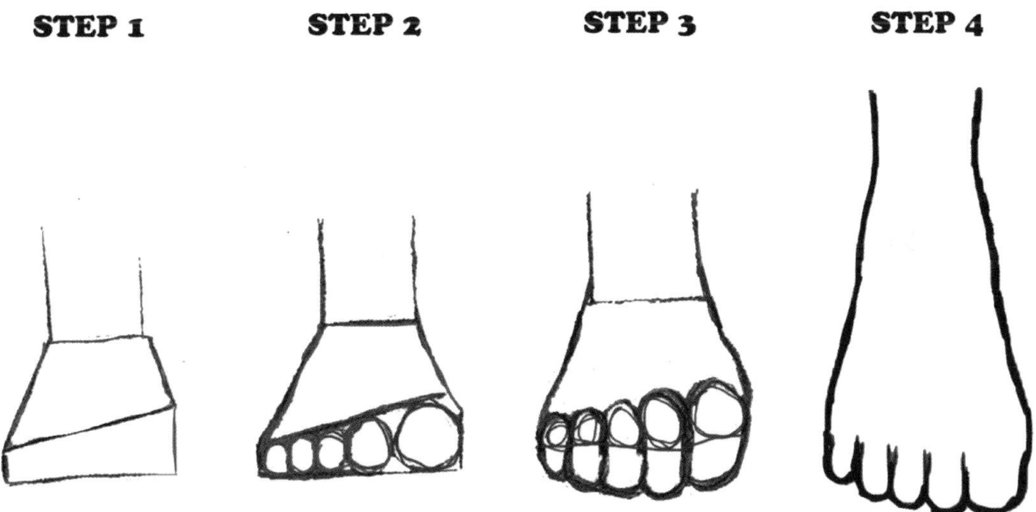

Side of Foot

To make it easy for you I have divided the anime foot into 4 simple shapes. Follow the steps below to learn how to create the side of your anime foot.

STEP 1

STEP 2

STEP 3

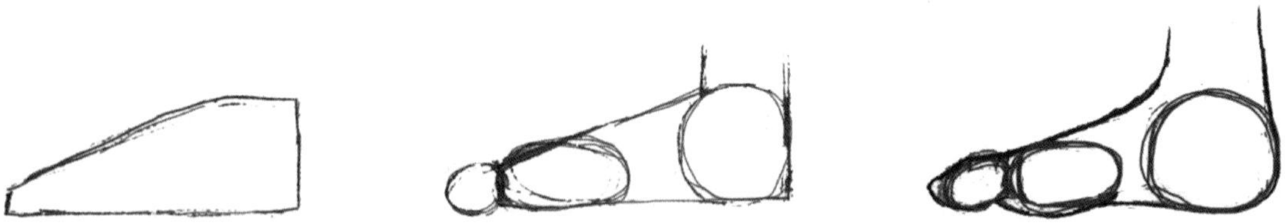

YOU ARE STRONG!!!

Clothing

This is my favorite chapter! Creating the clothing! I love making anime clothing! In this chapter I will teach you some tips and tricks to drawing your anime clothing. You can look at any type of clothing to get inspiration on what to draw. I like to get inspiration from various clothing stores on the Internet or in clothing magazines. When I find the outfit I want to use I like to add my own personal customization to create a new design.

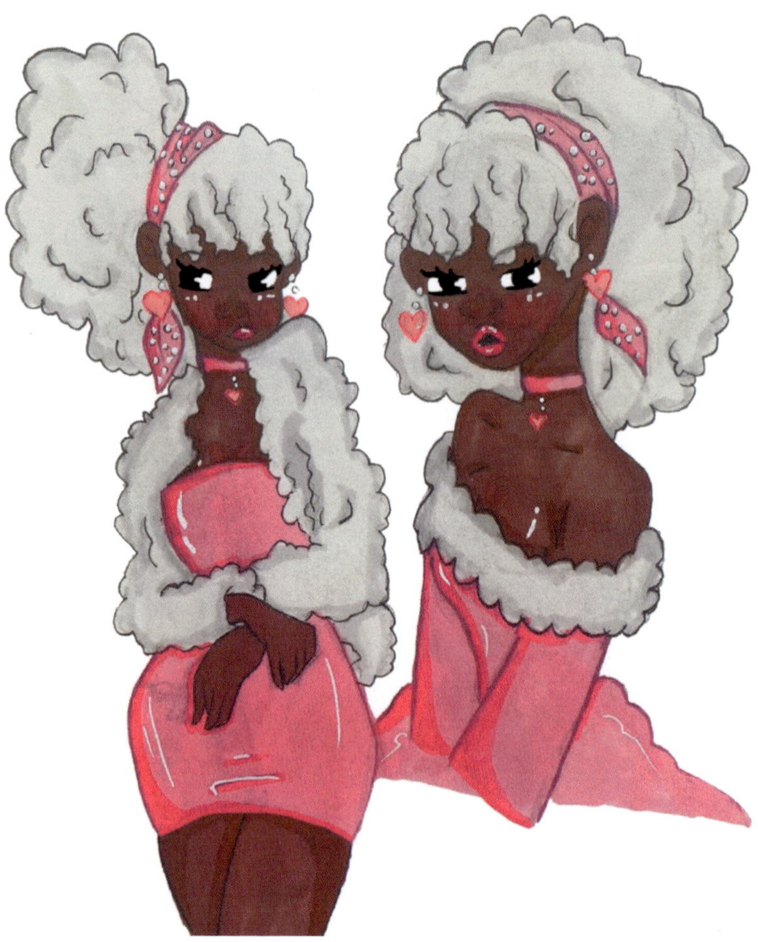

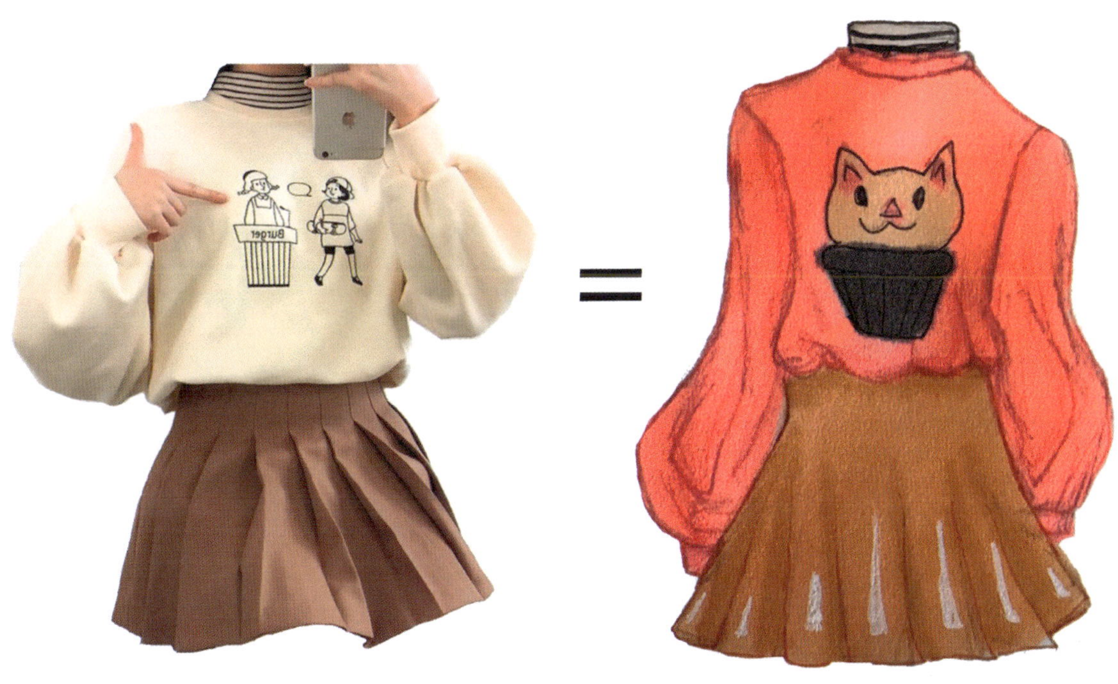
Burger

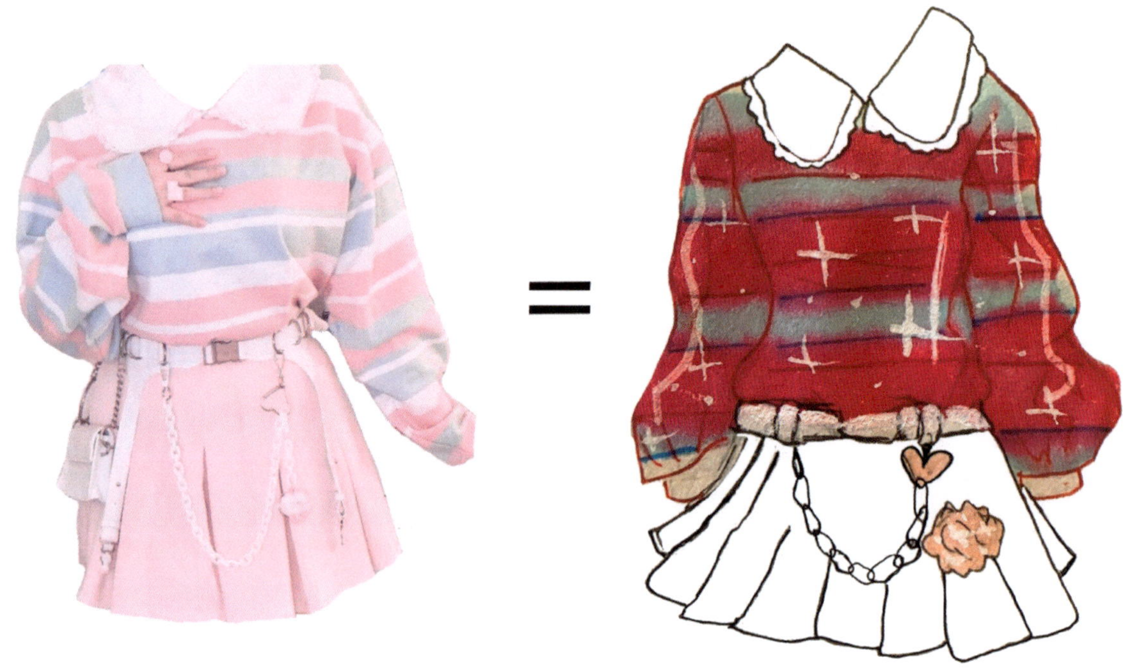

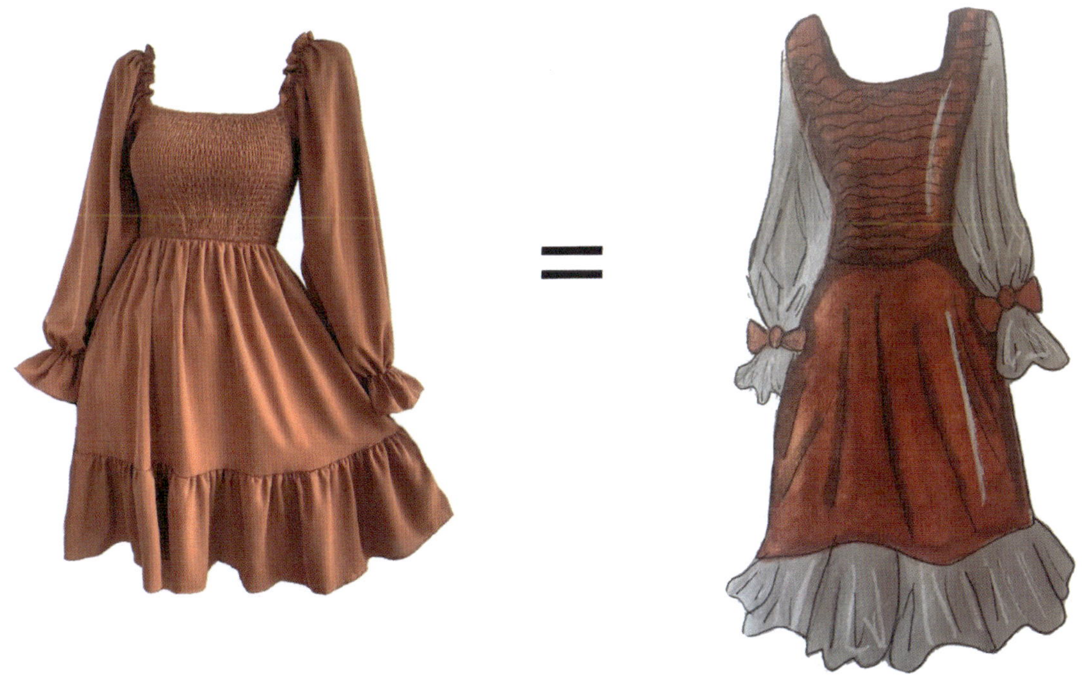

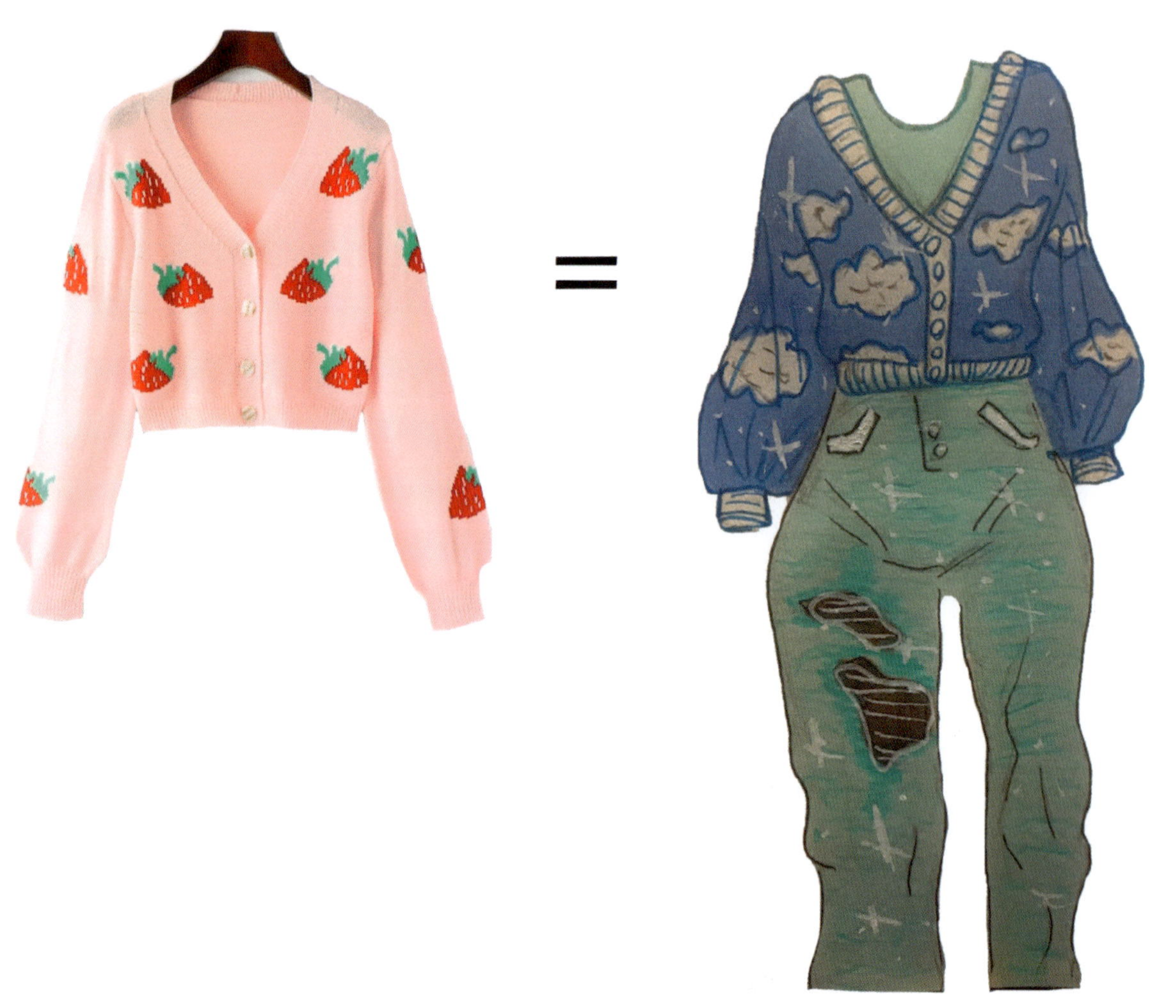

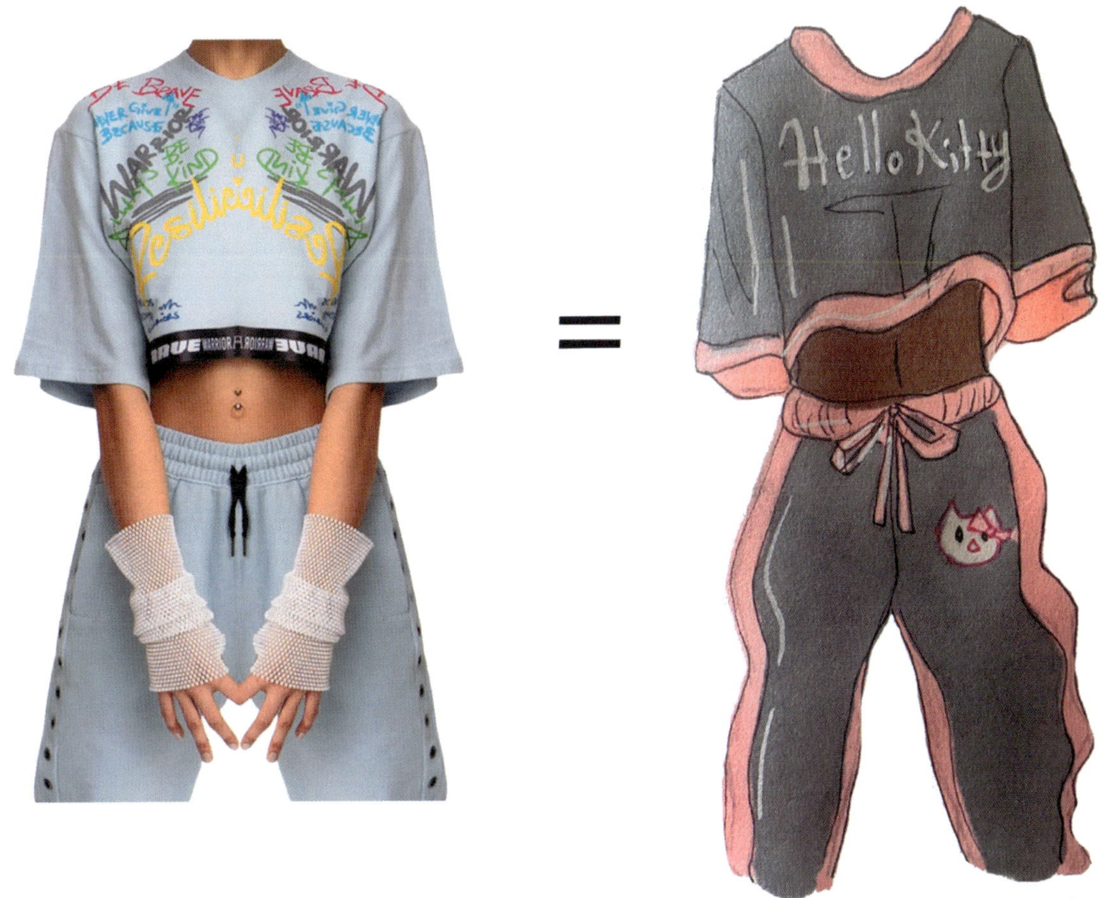
Hello Kitty

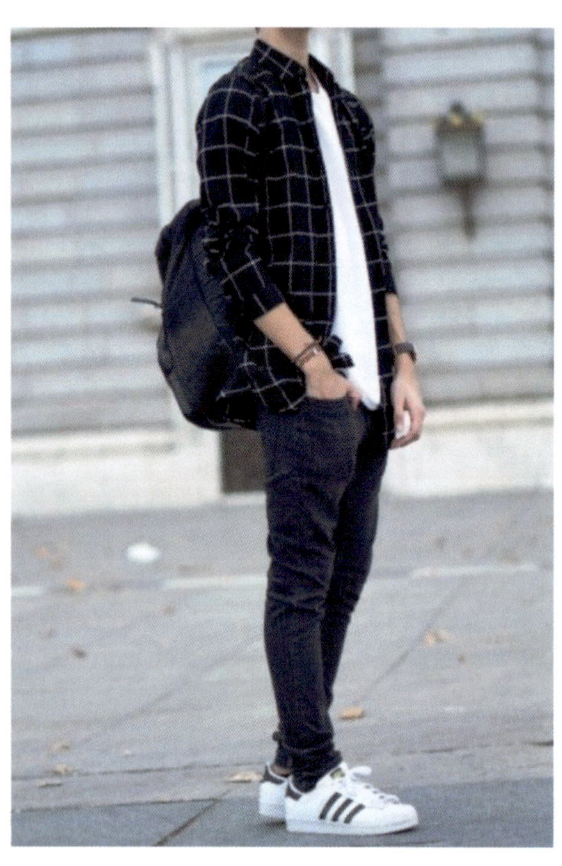

=

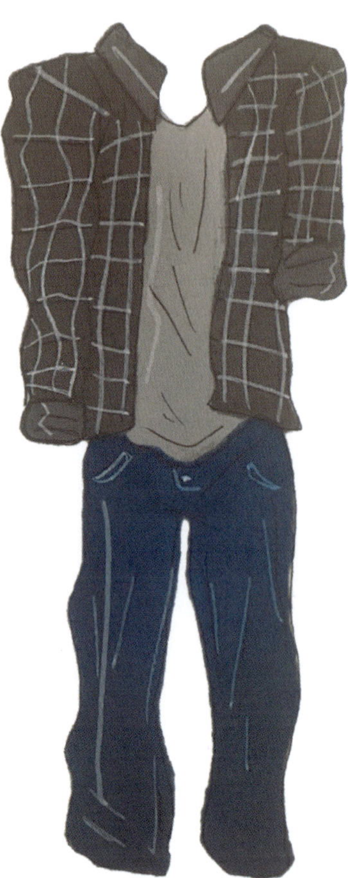

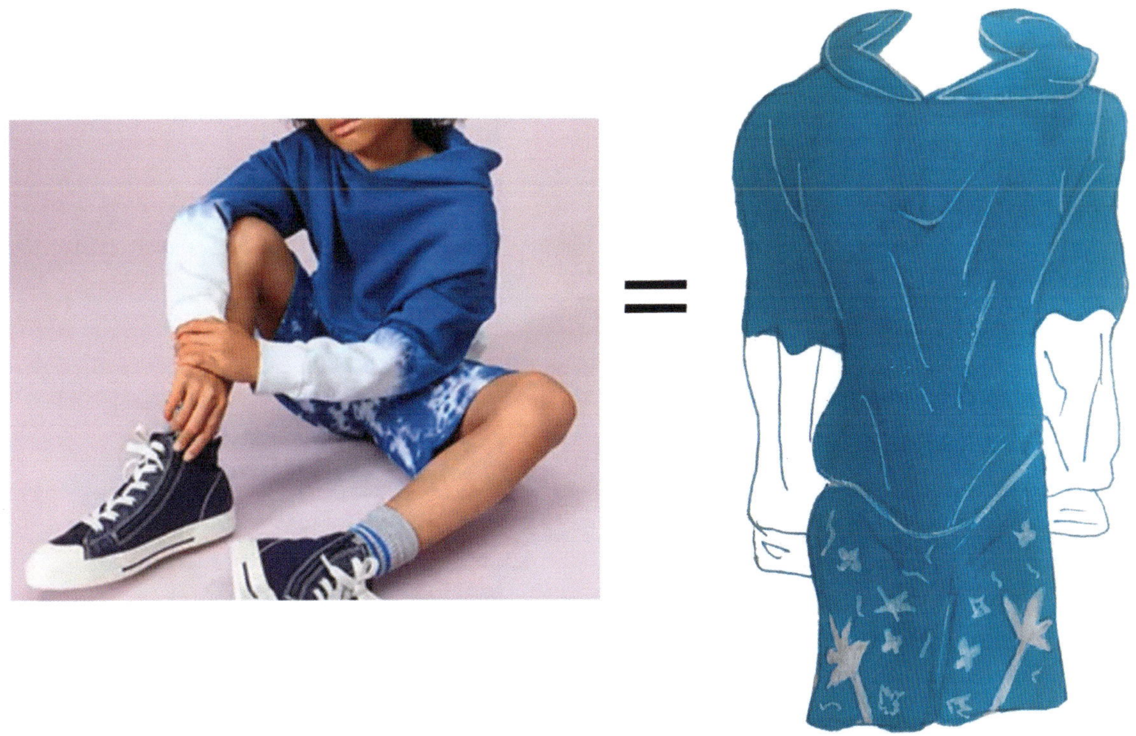

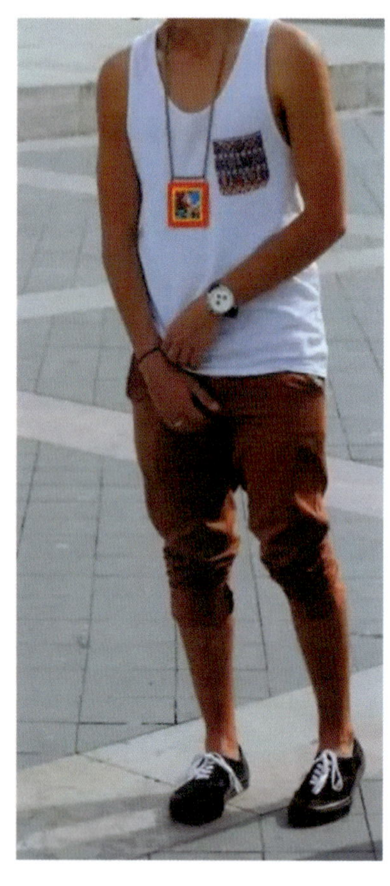

=

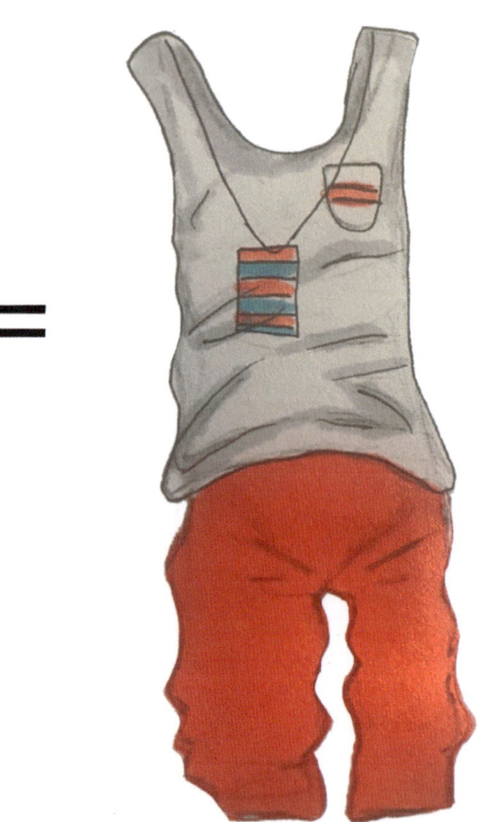

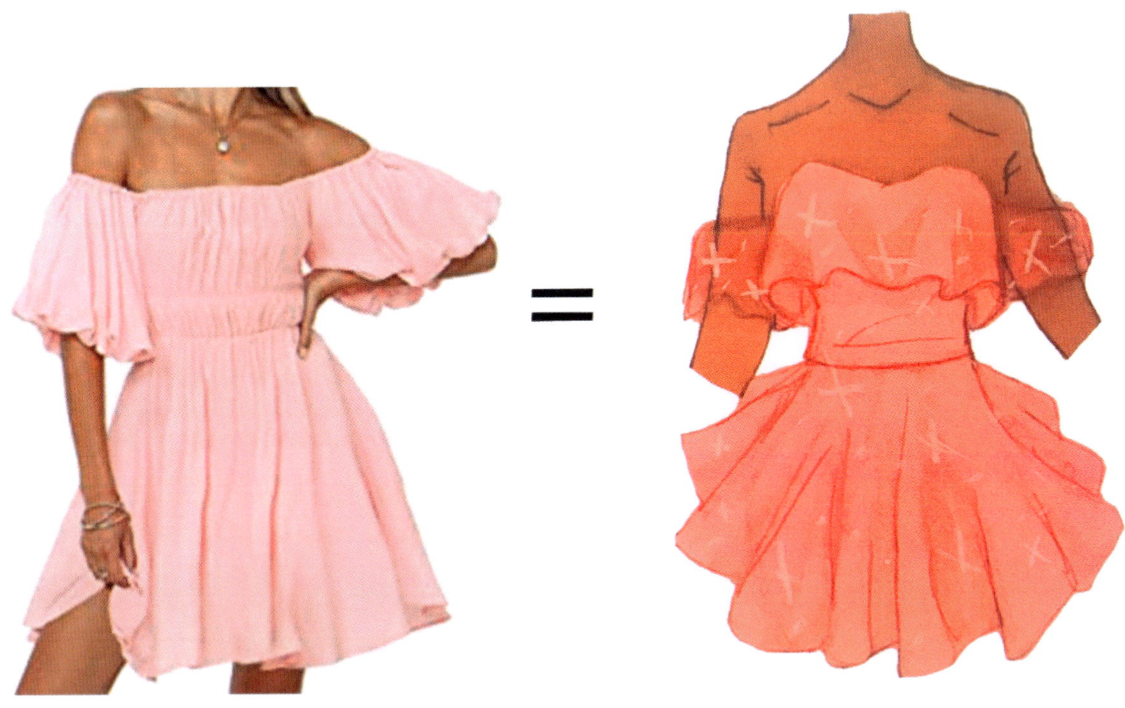

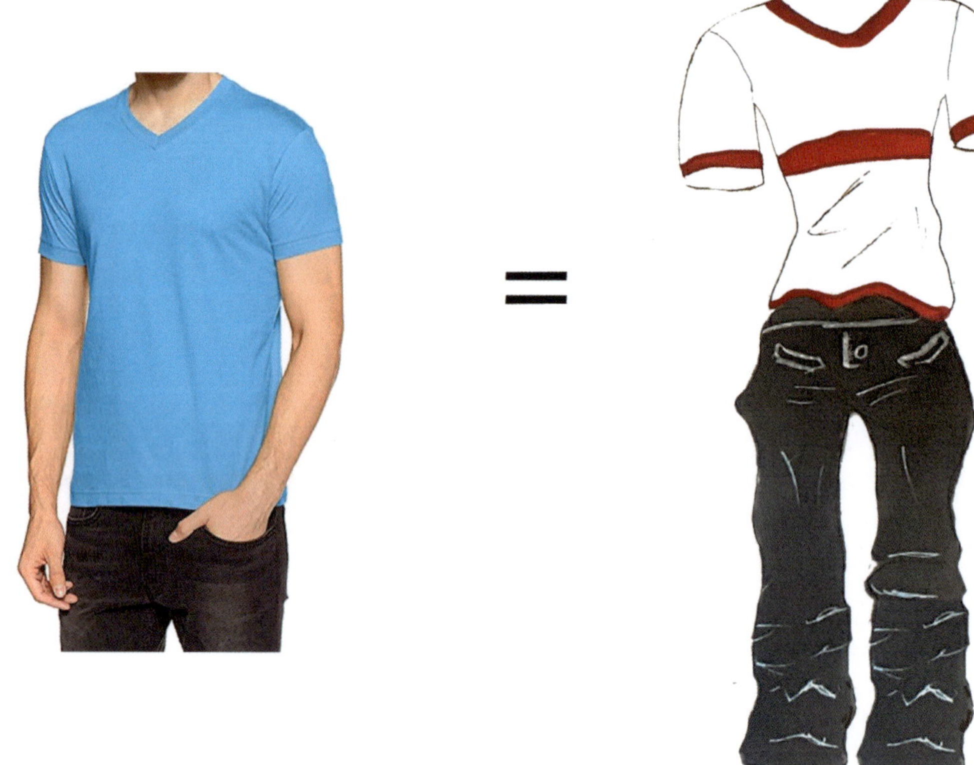

Shoes

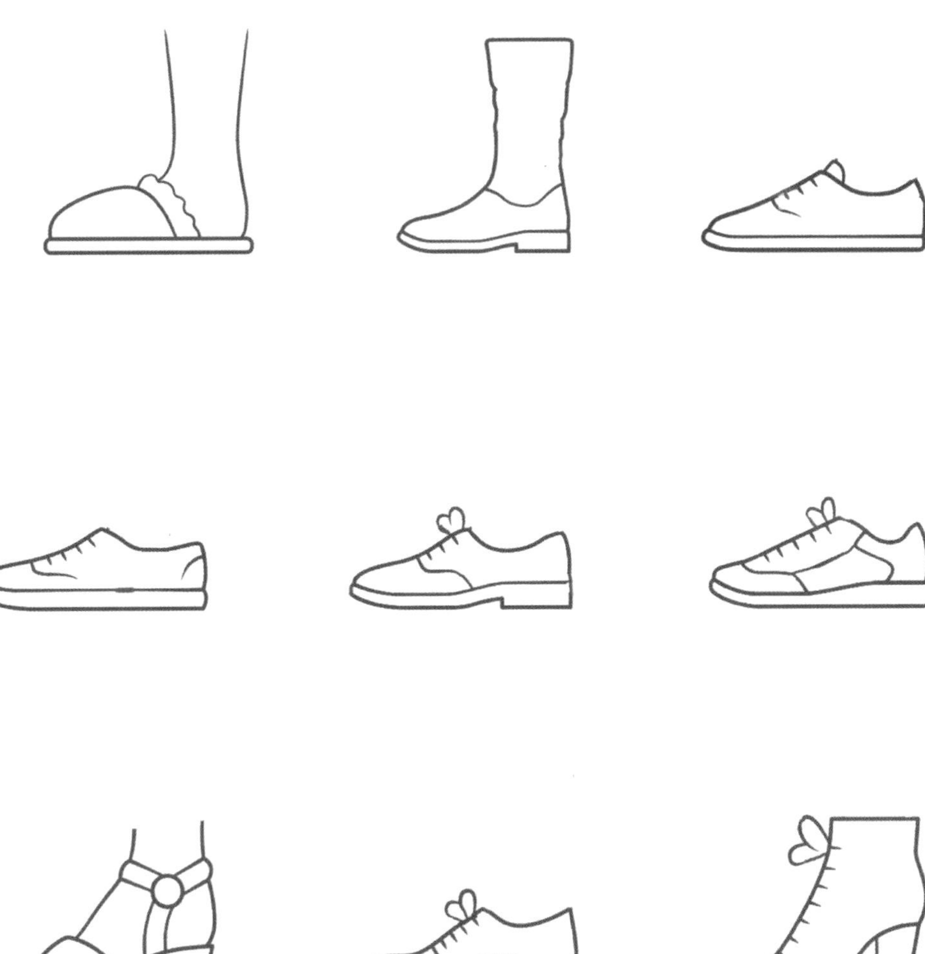

Poses

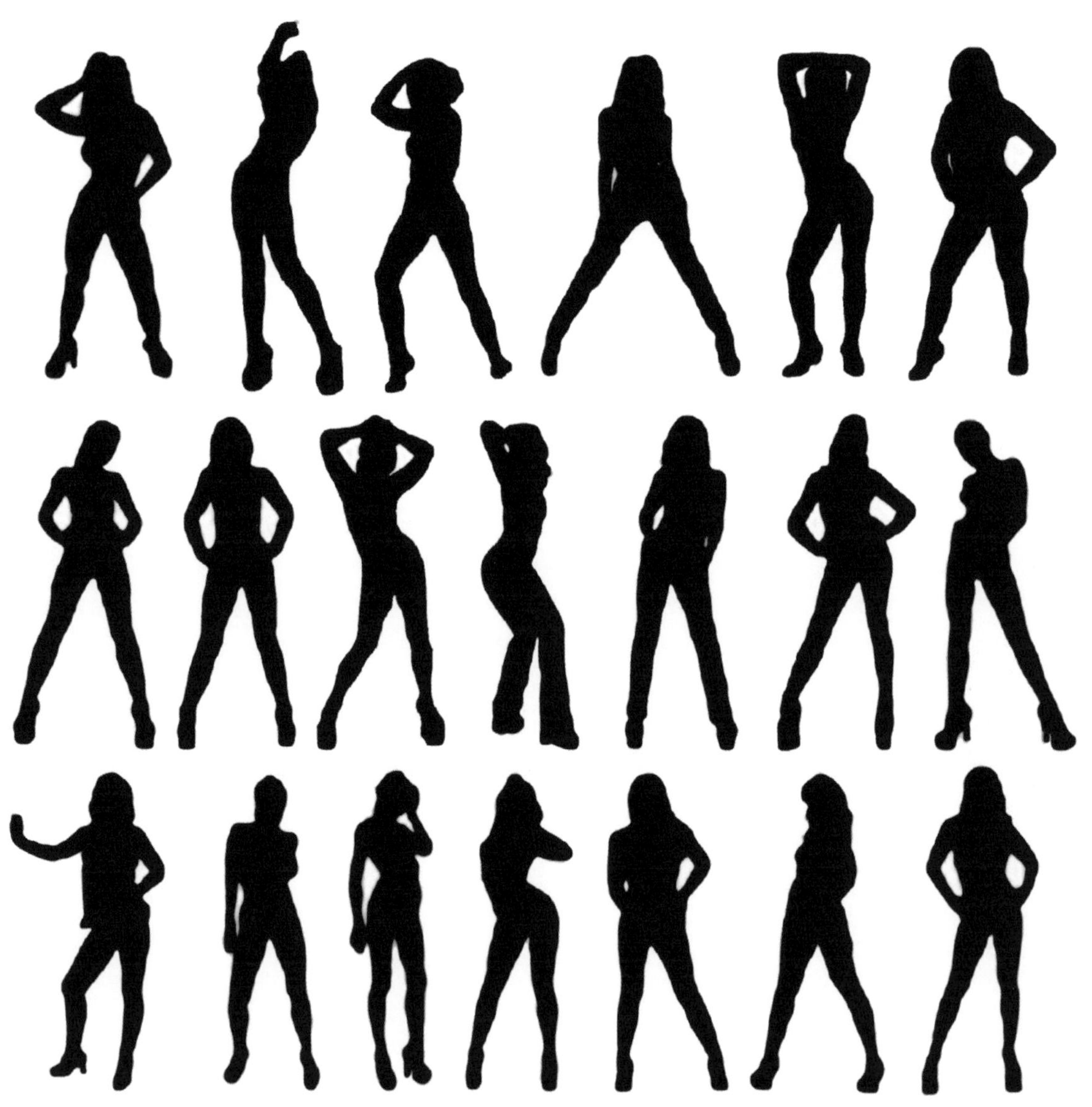

Poses

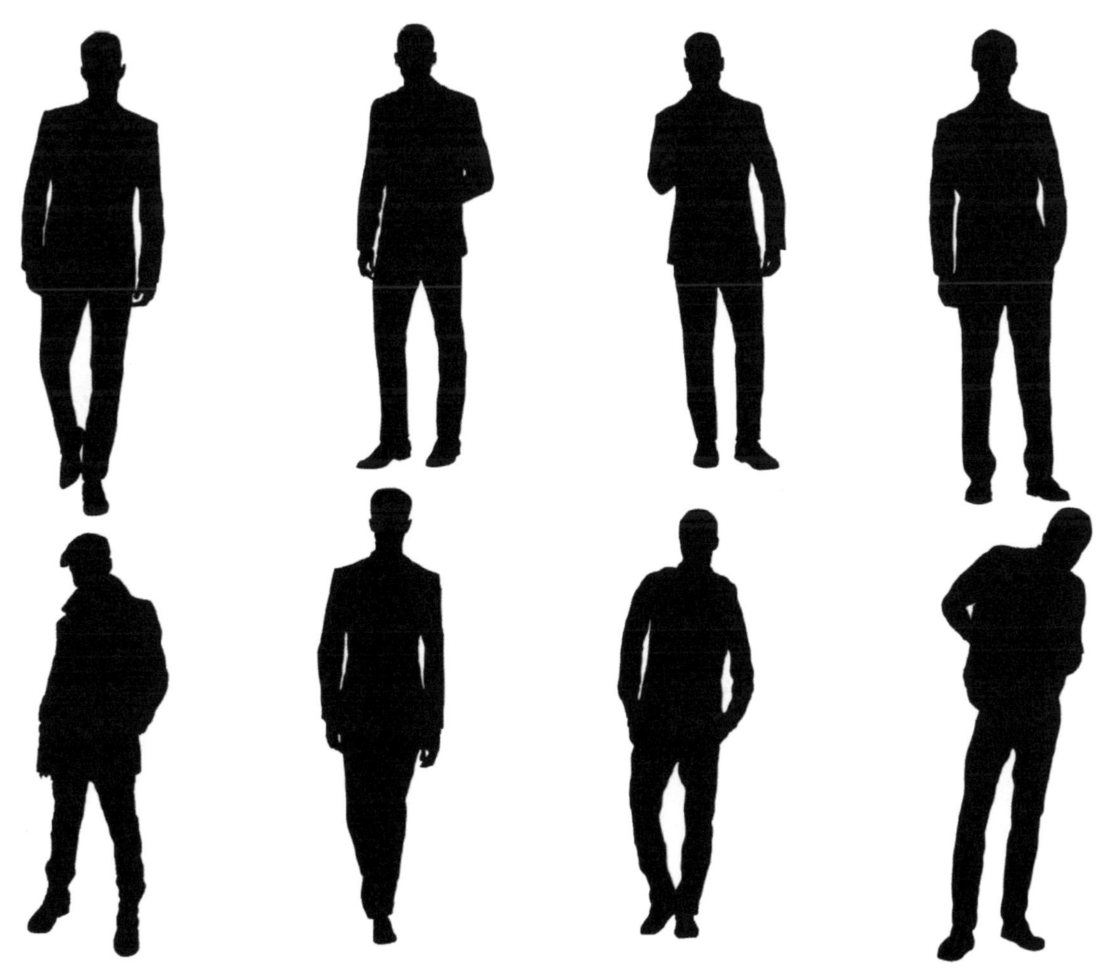

YOU ARE RESILIENT!!!

Outlining and Coloring your Anime

Finally your here! The final part to completing your anime is coloring! In this section I will teach you how I color my anime. You will utilize the shading and blending skills you learned in the earlier chapters. You will need your alcohol markers. Let's get started!

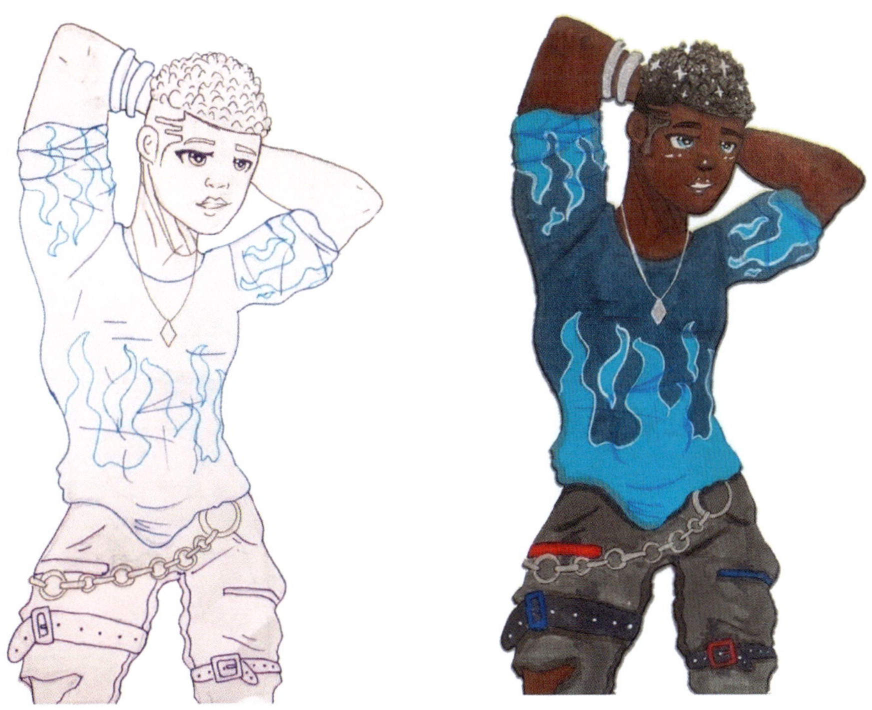

Outlining

Now it's time to work on finalizing your anime! It's time to Outline! Before you outline make sure you lightly erase your penciled in anime. You have to do this to prepare it for outlining and coloring. If you don't lightly erase, you will see all of the pencil sketch marks in your final drawing. You will need your finepoint pens to outline. You can use all black pens for the outlines, or different colors. ...NICE RIGHT! Lets get started!

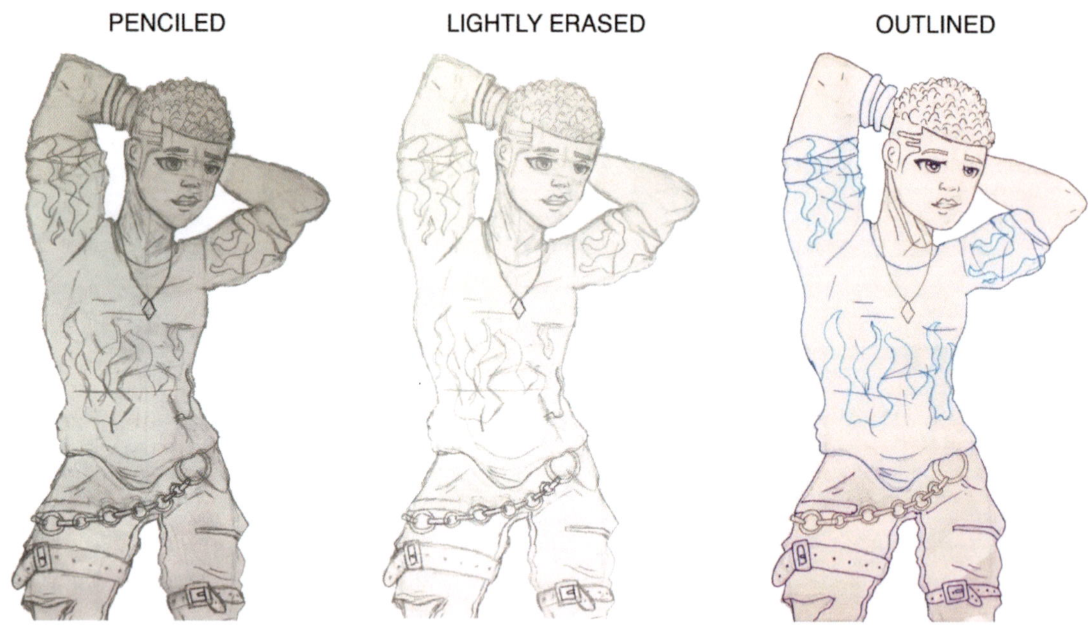

Outlining

After you have drawn your anime and erased the pencil lines it's time to outline. Outlining is the first step before coloring your anime!

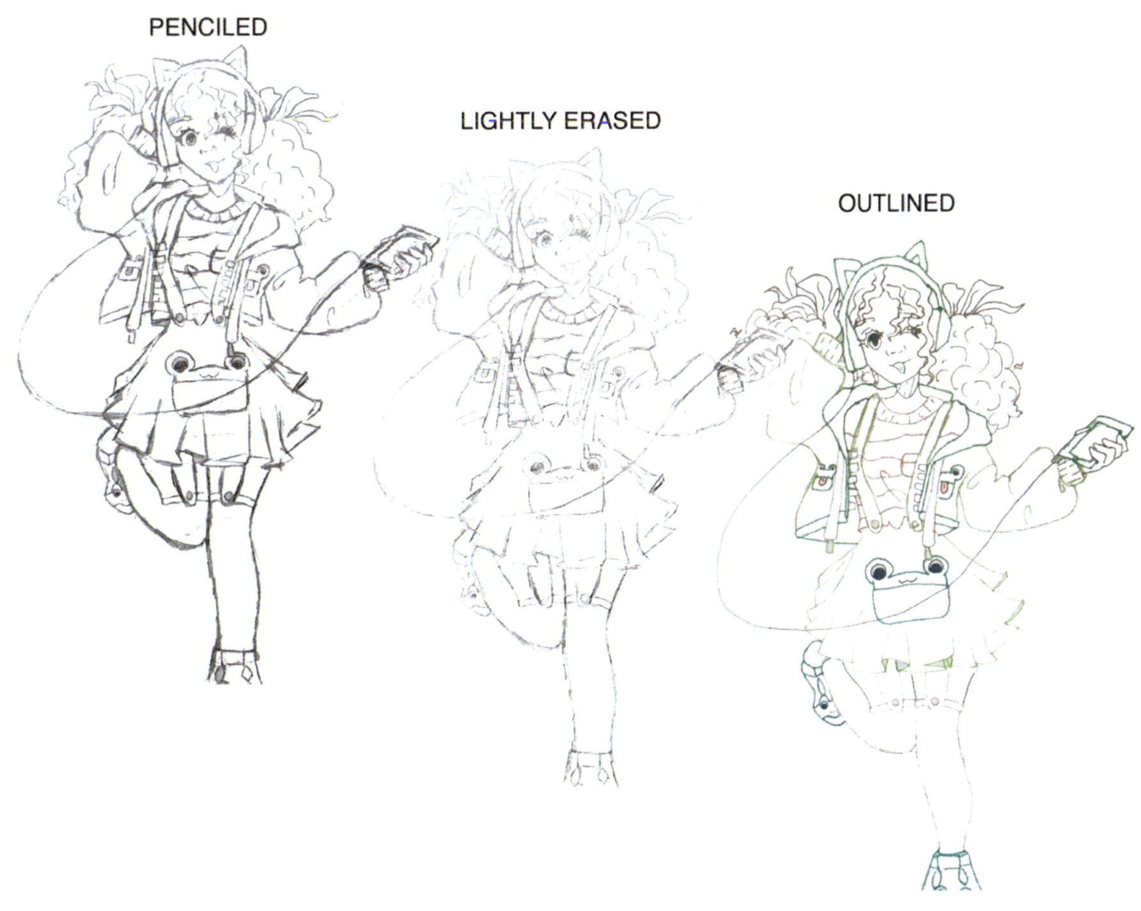

Coloring your Anime

Finally your here! The final part to completing your anime, Coloring! In this section I will teach you how to color your anime. You will utilize the shading and blending skills you learned in the earlier chapters. You will need your alcohol markers. Let's get started!

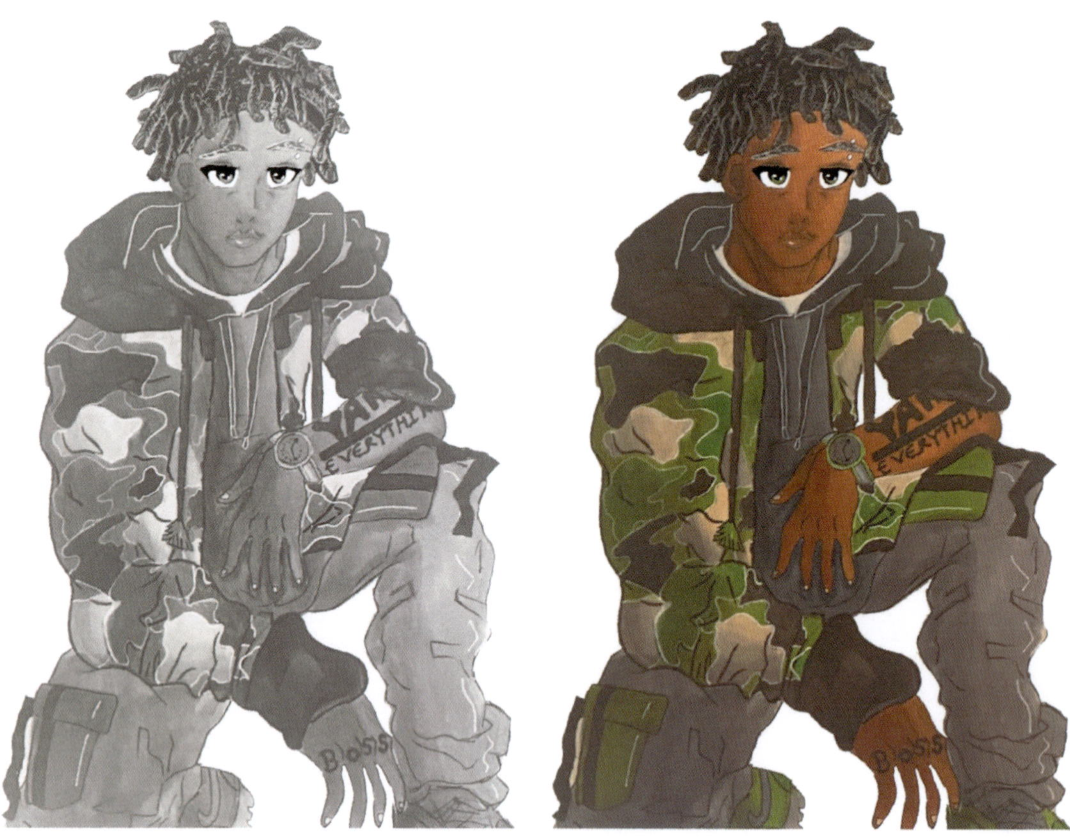

To color your drawing you must have several shades of the color you want to use. As you can see below I used 4 different shades of brown on my characters face. I created a light source on my character. Remember A light source is the direction from which light originates. As you can see below the front of his face is lighter and as I shade farther away from the light source his face gets darker. I also used my colorless blender (alcohol marker tool) to blend the different shades of color together.

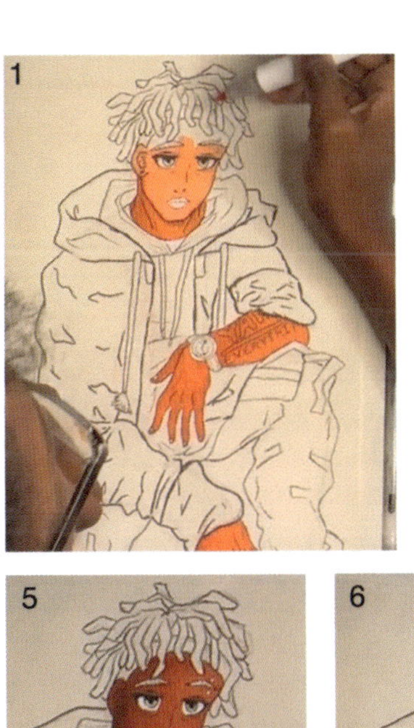

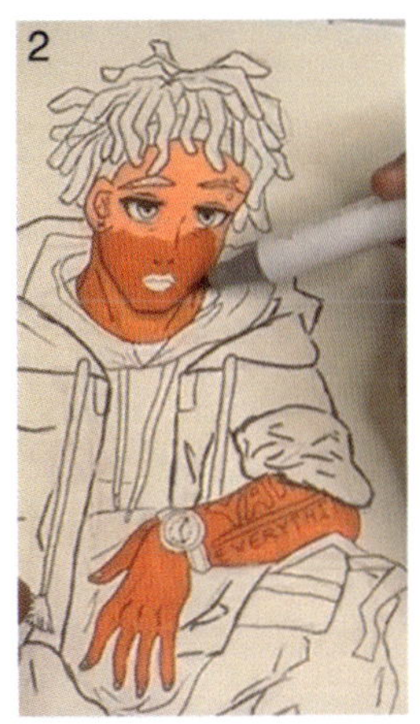

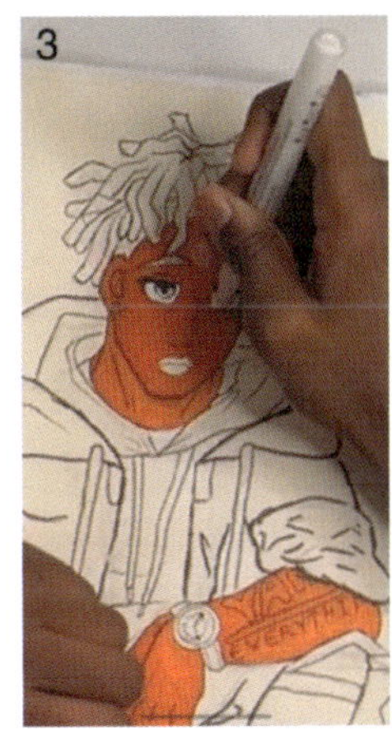

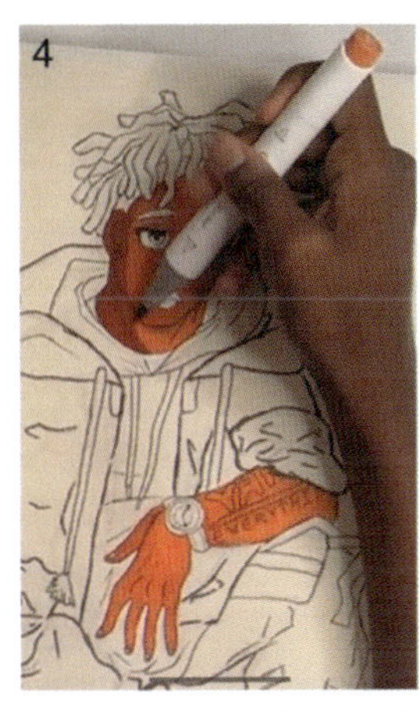

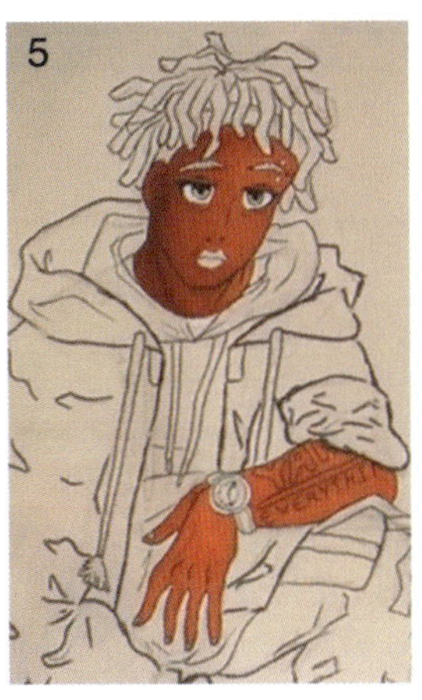

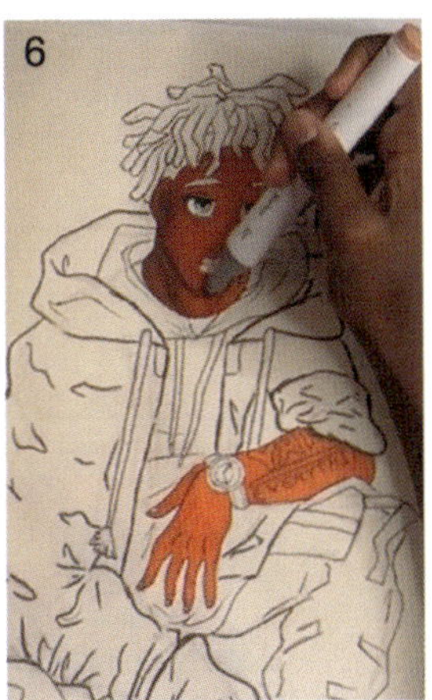

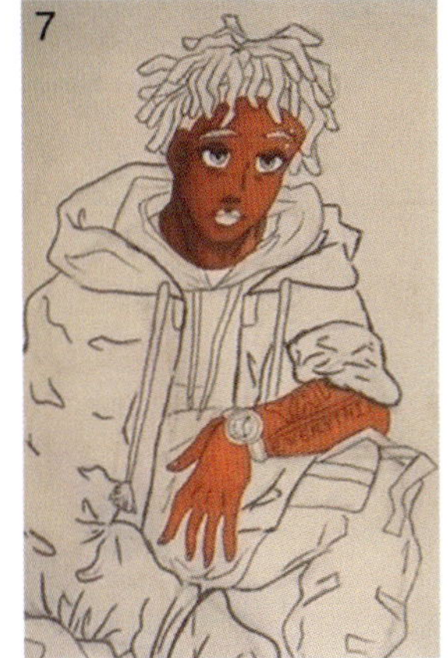

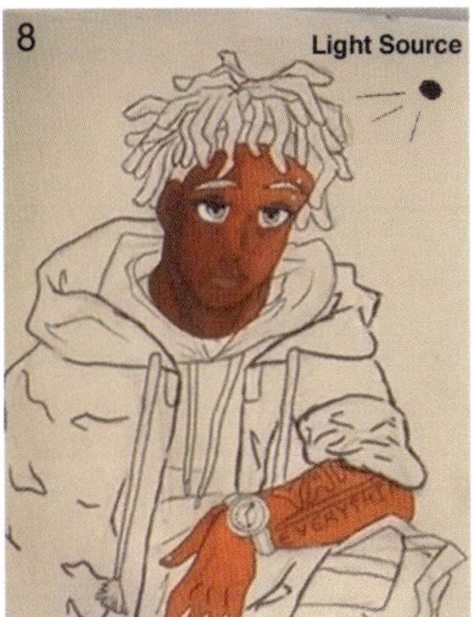

YOU CAN BE SUCCESSFUL!!!

Tutorials

You've made it to the last section of my book, the Tutorials! I've created a few OC's (original characters) with step-by-step instructions for you to follow. Use all of my techniques in the book to help you recreate my Anime characters. Enjoy!

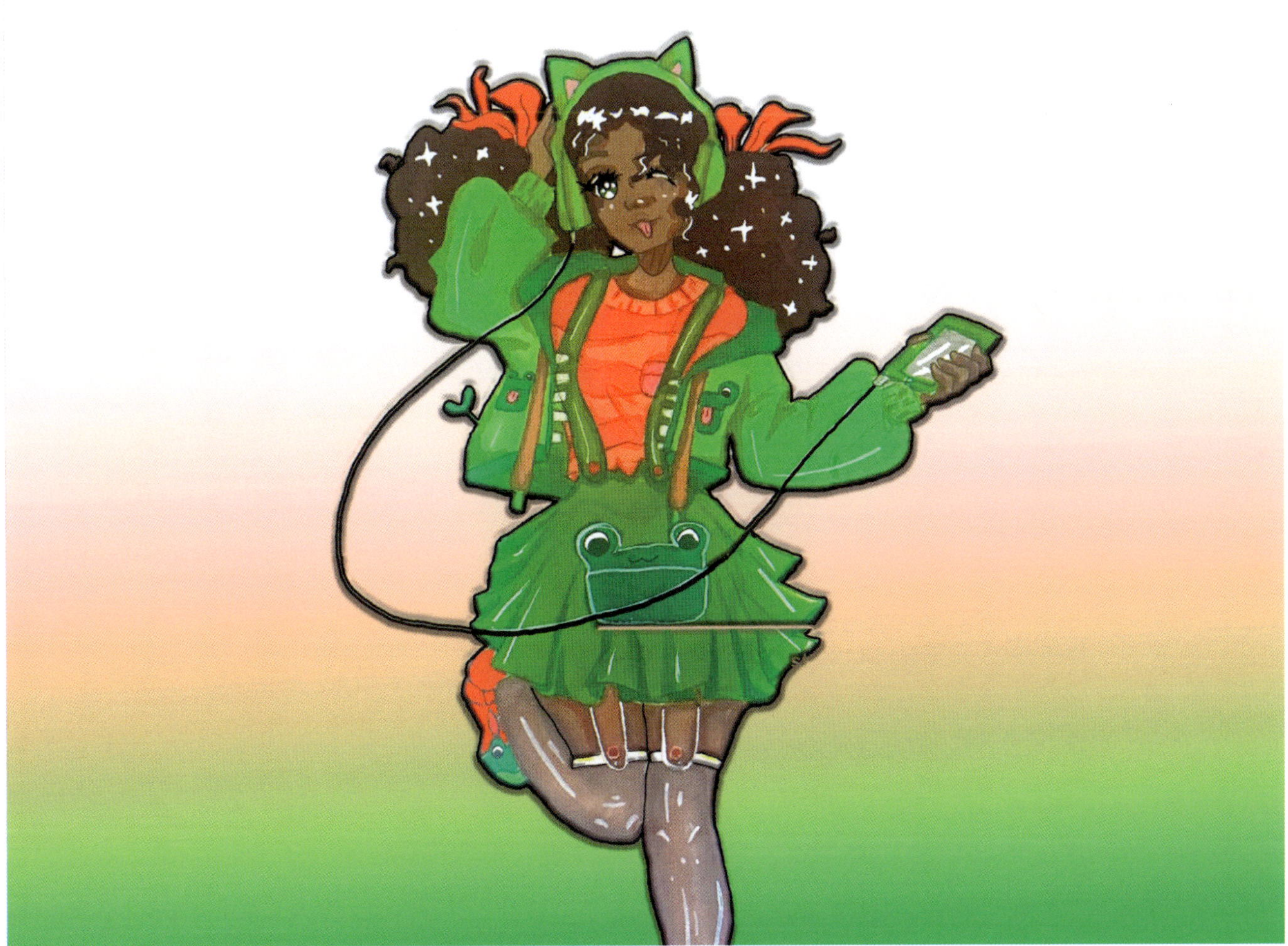

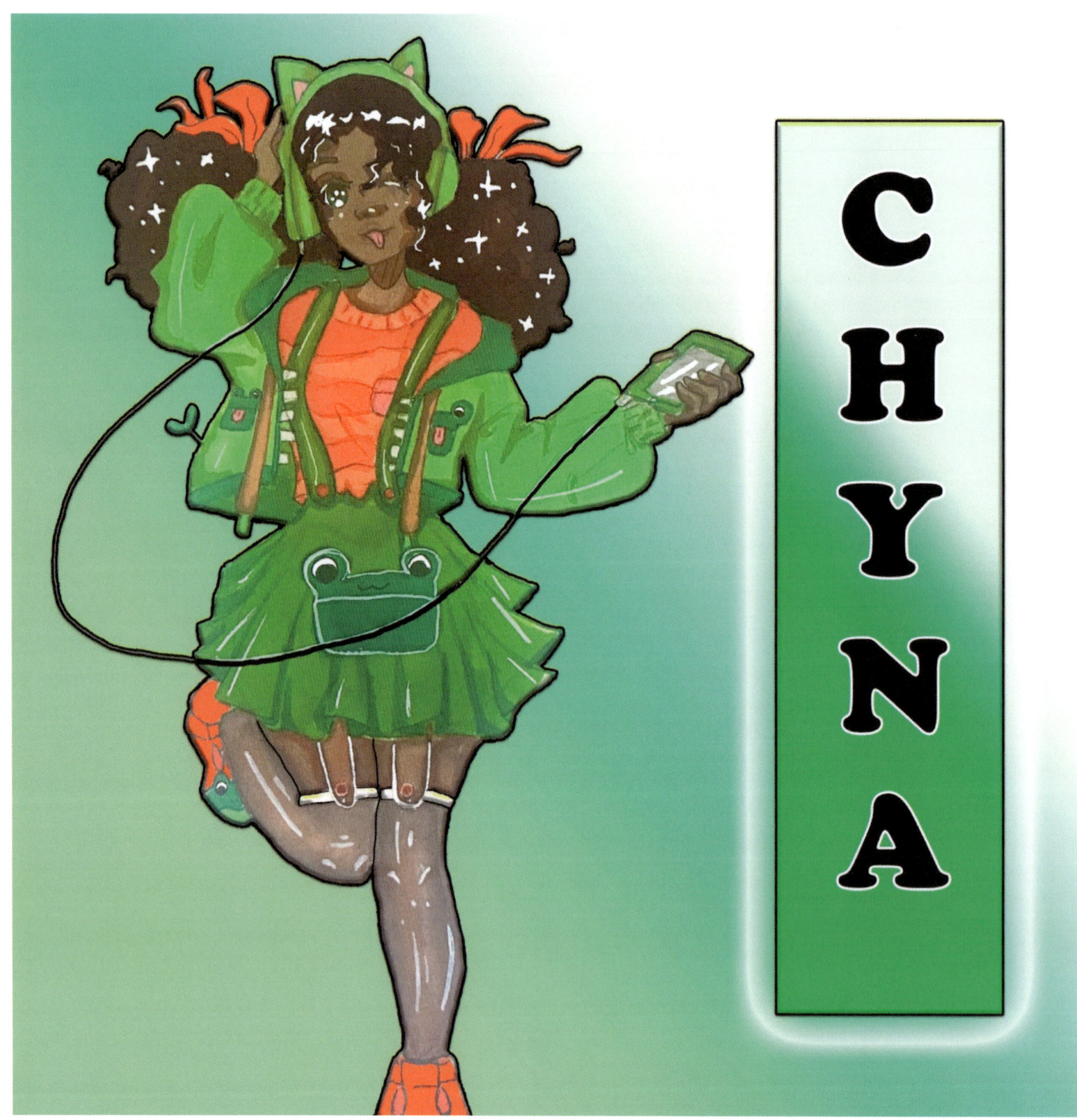
CHYNA

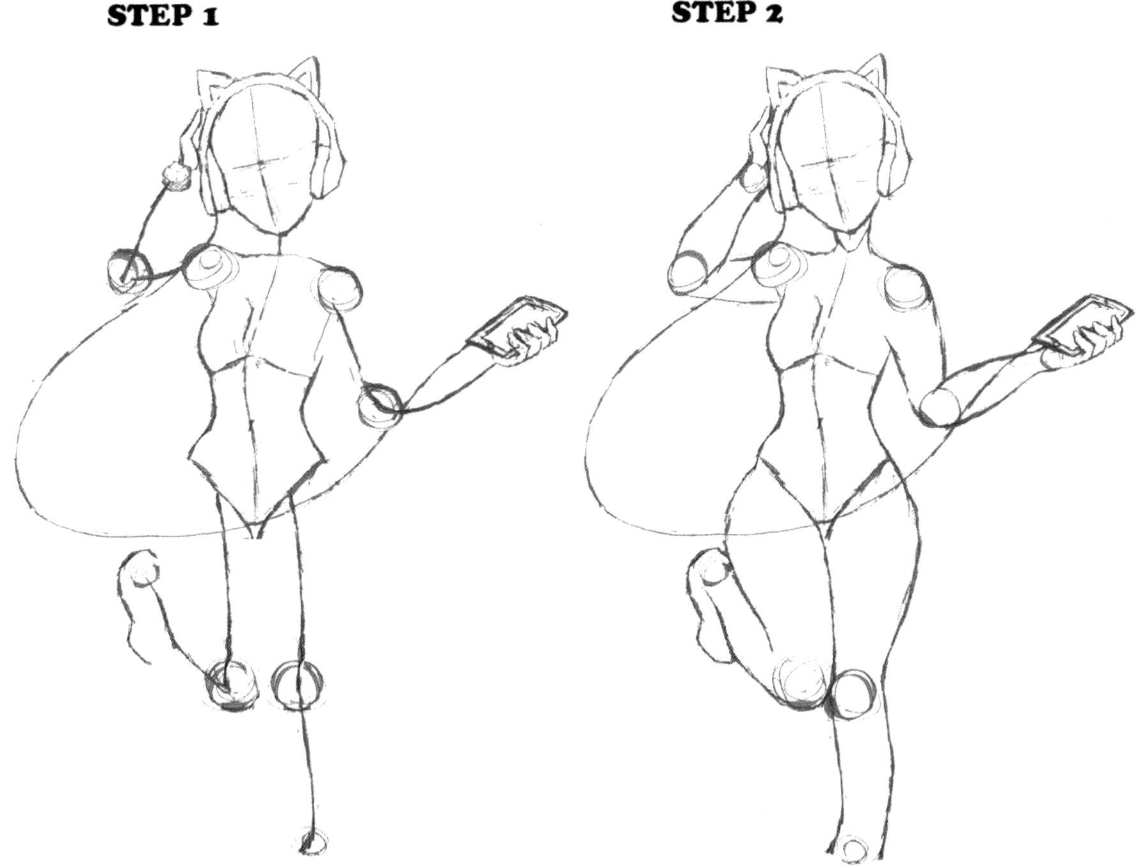
STEP 1
STEP 2

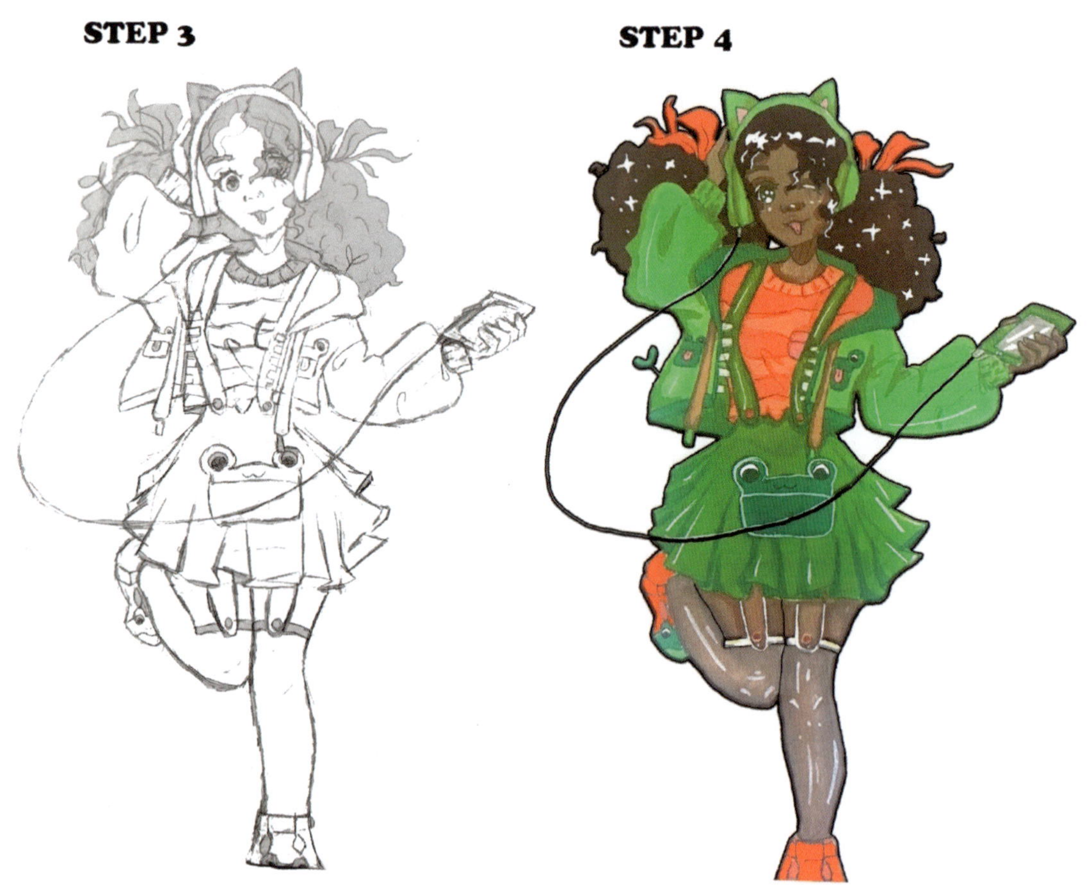
STEP 3
STEP 4

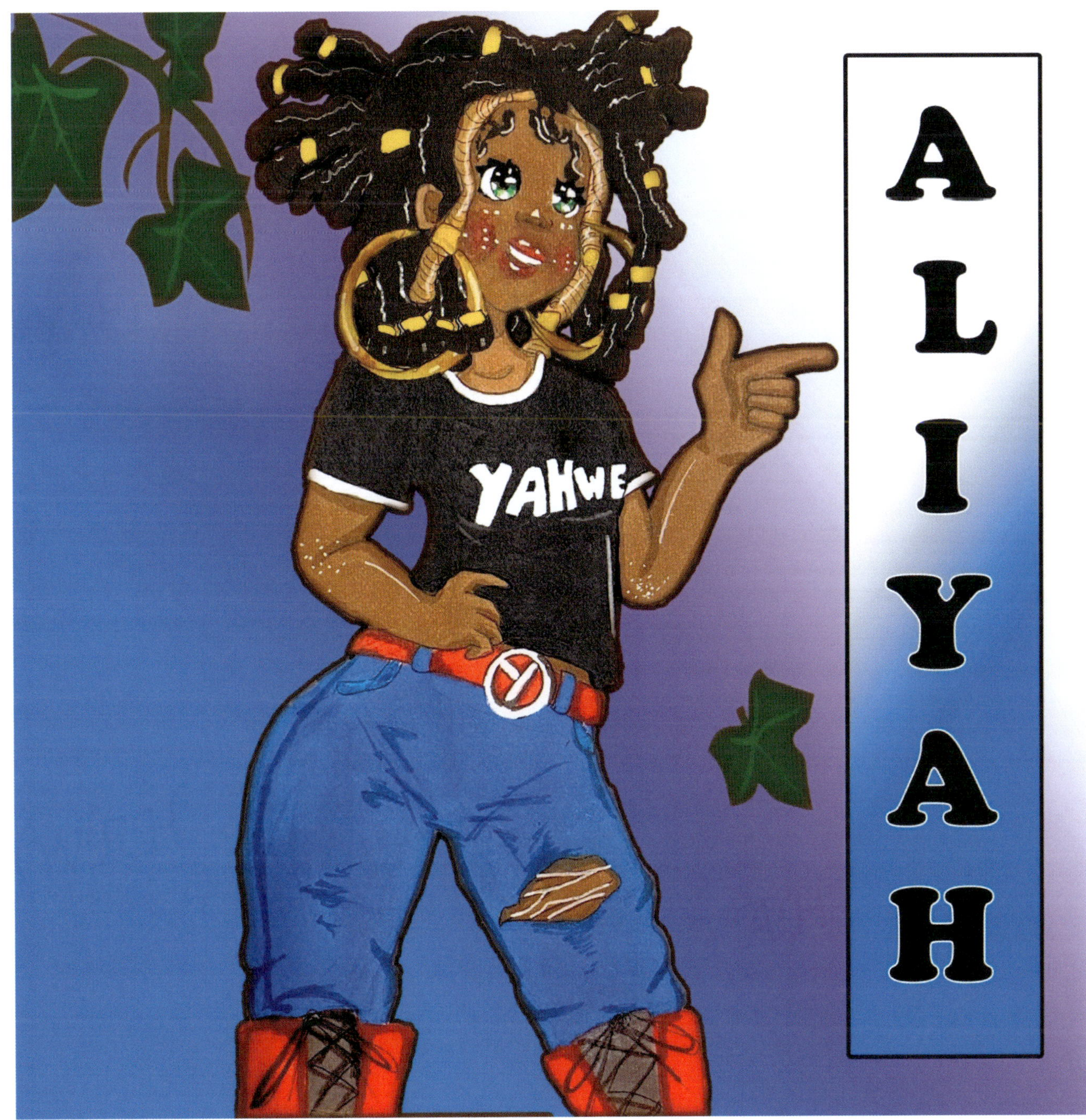
YAHWE
ALIYAH

STEP 1

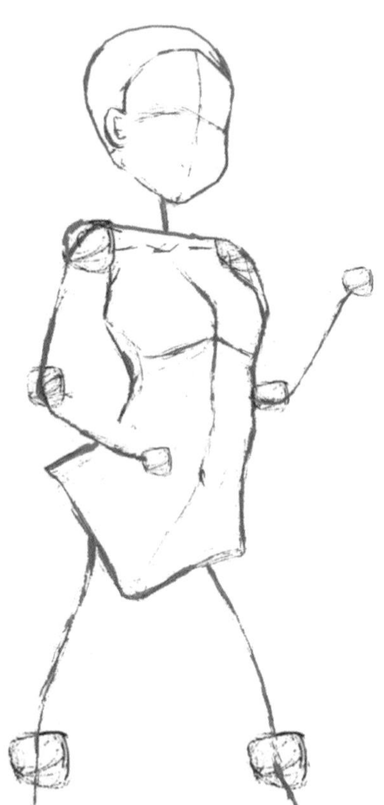

STEP 2

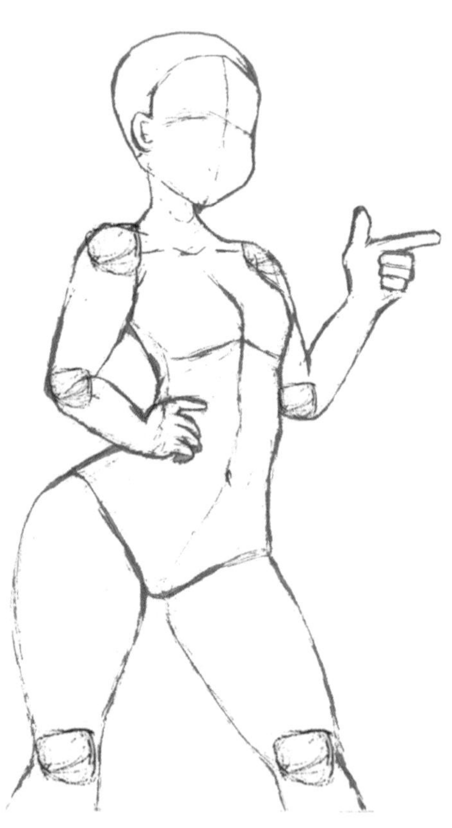

STEP 3

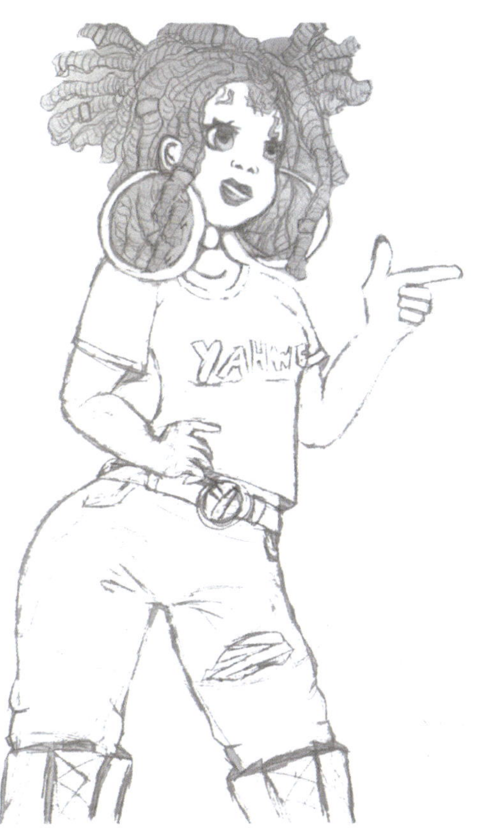

STEP 4

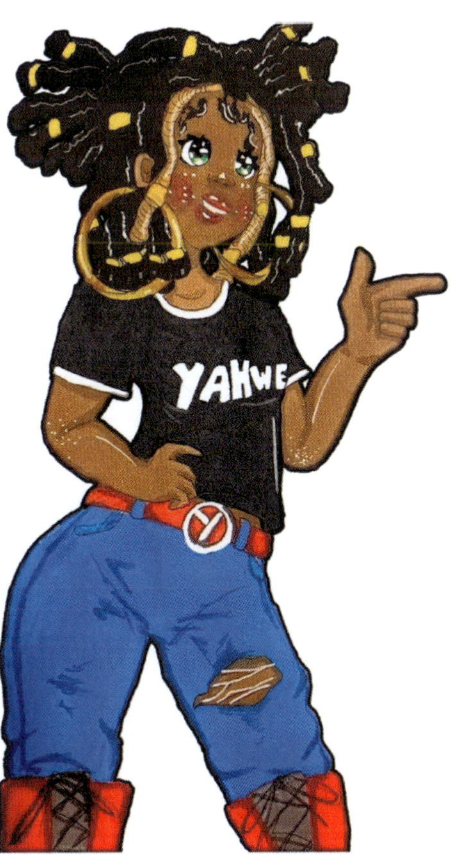

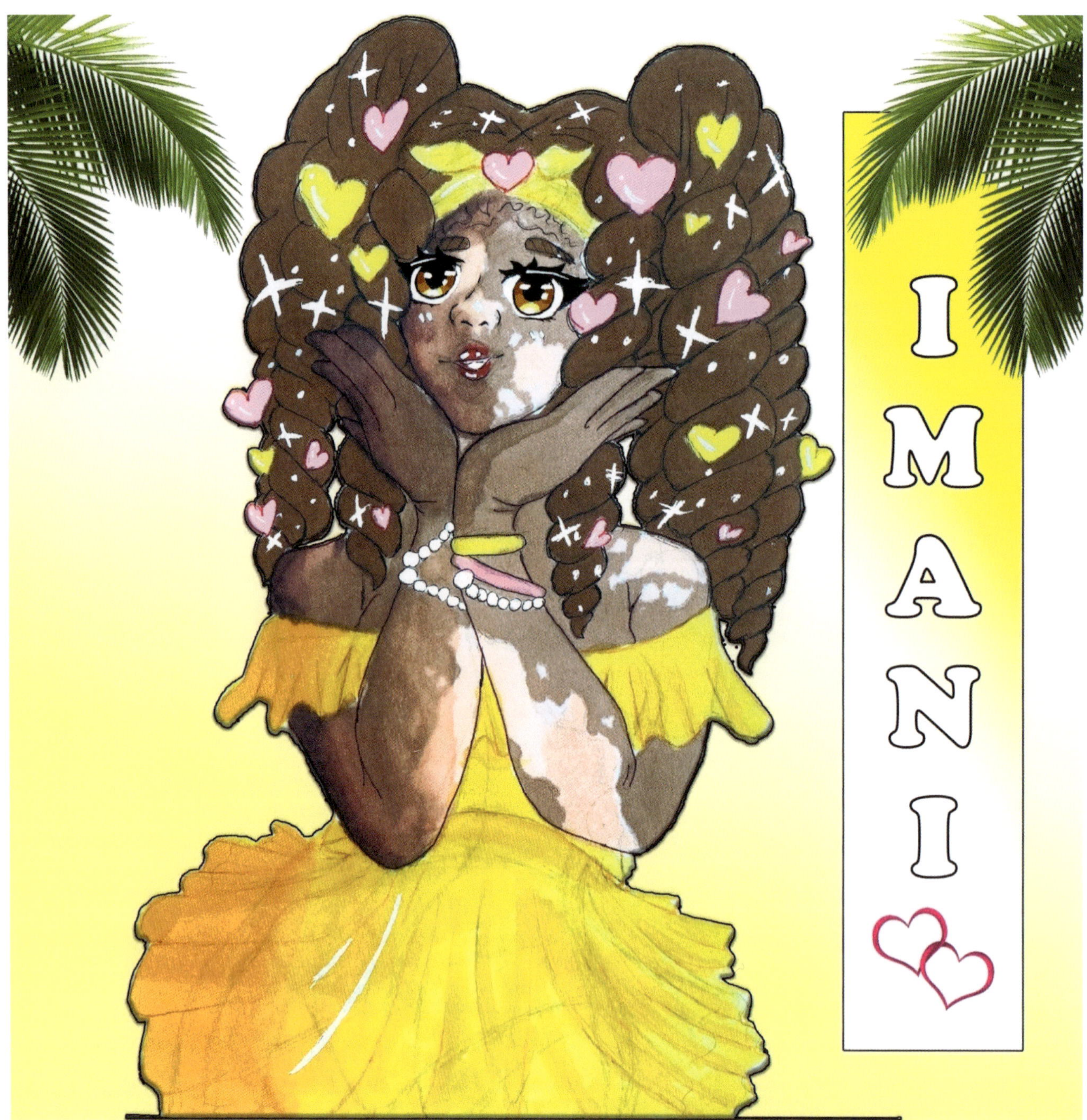
IMANI

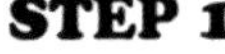

STEP 2

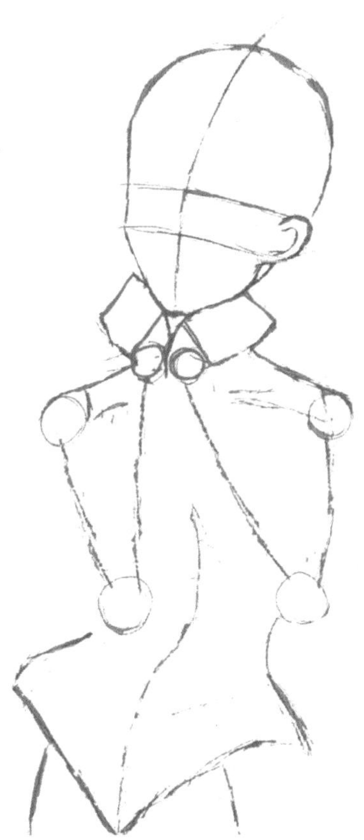

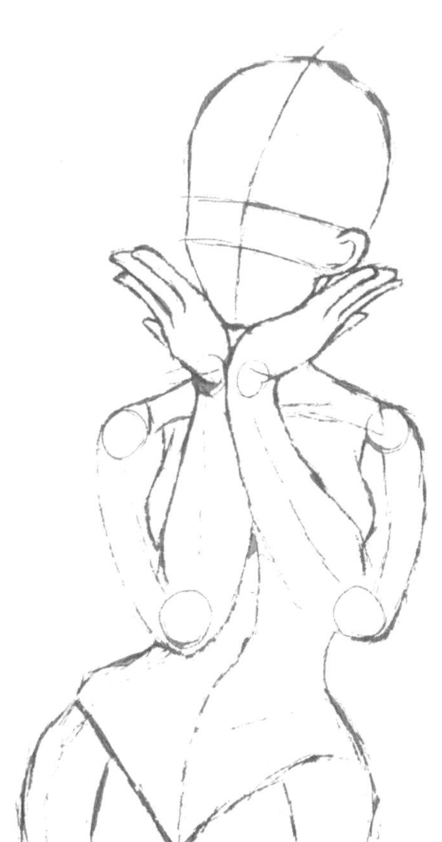

STEP 3

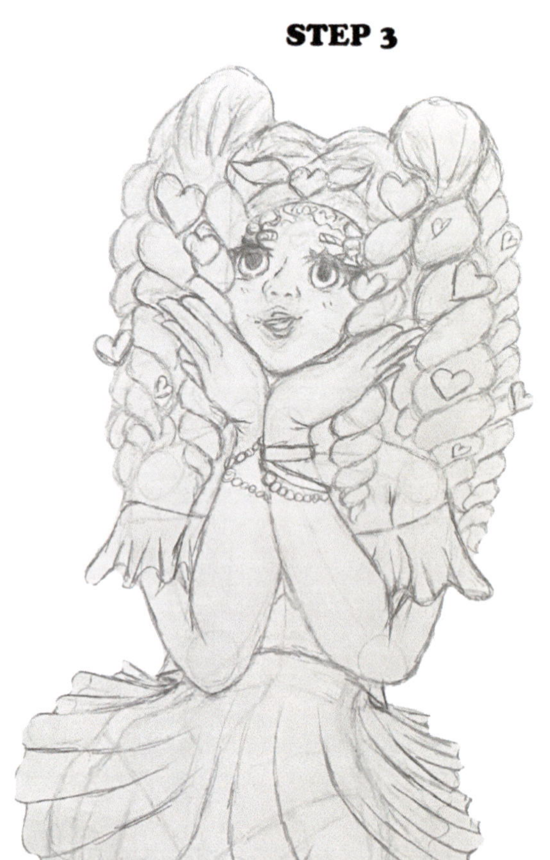

STEP 4

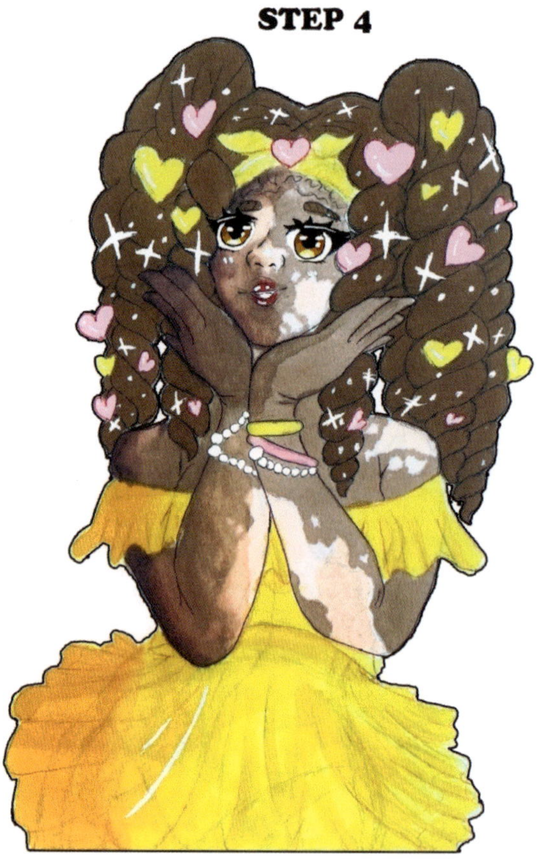

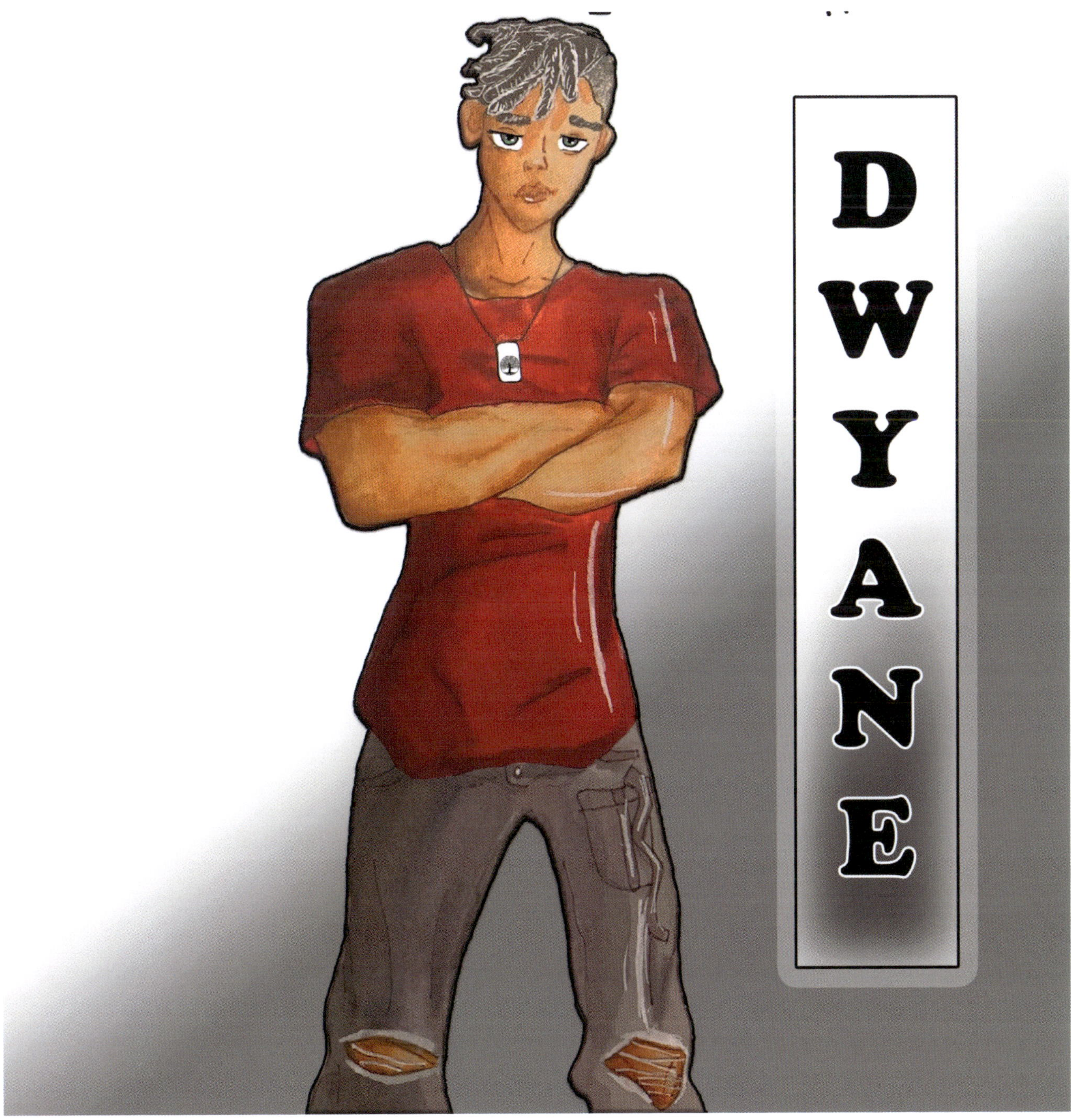
DWYANE

STEP 1

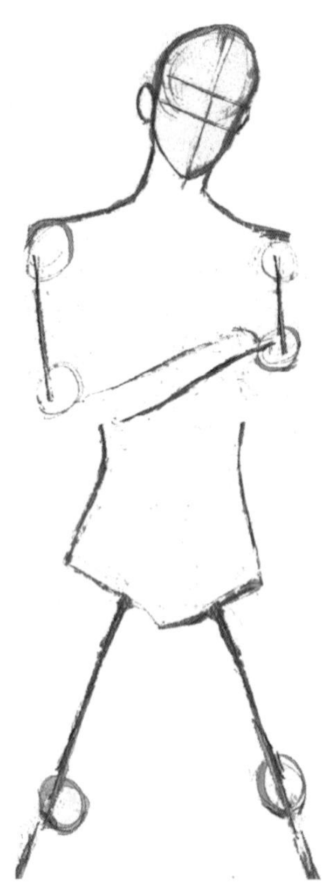

STEP 2

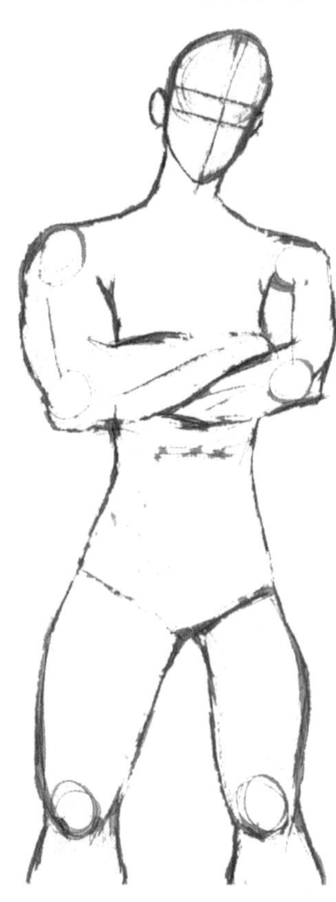

STEP 3

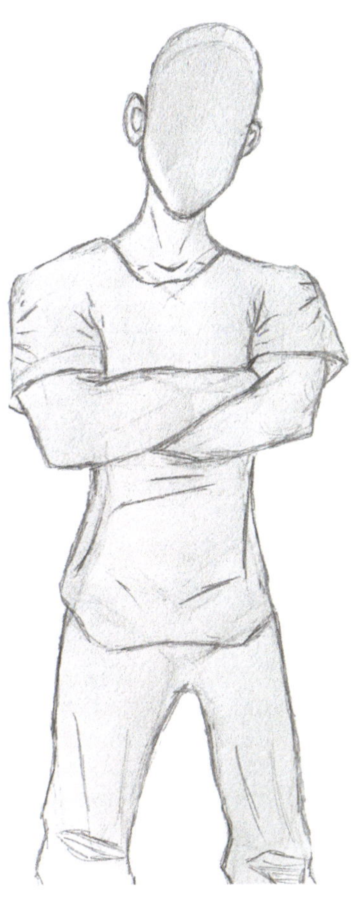

STEP 4

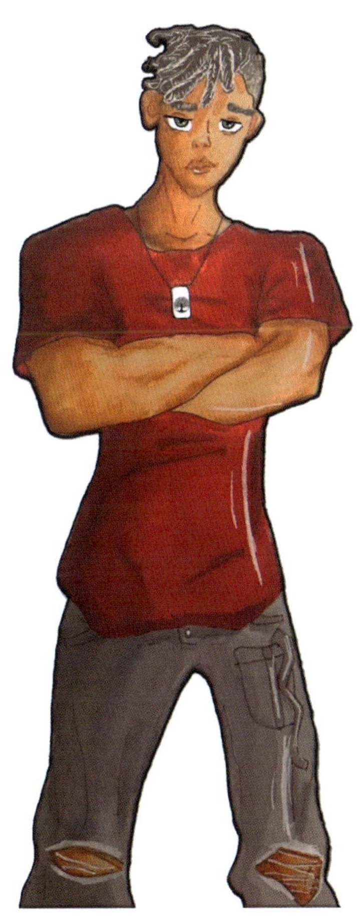

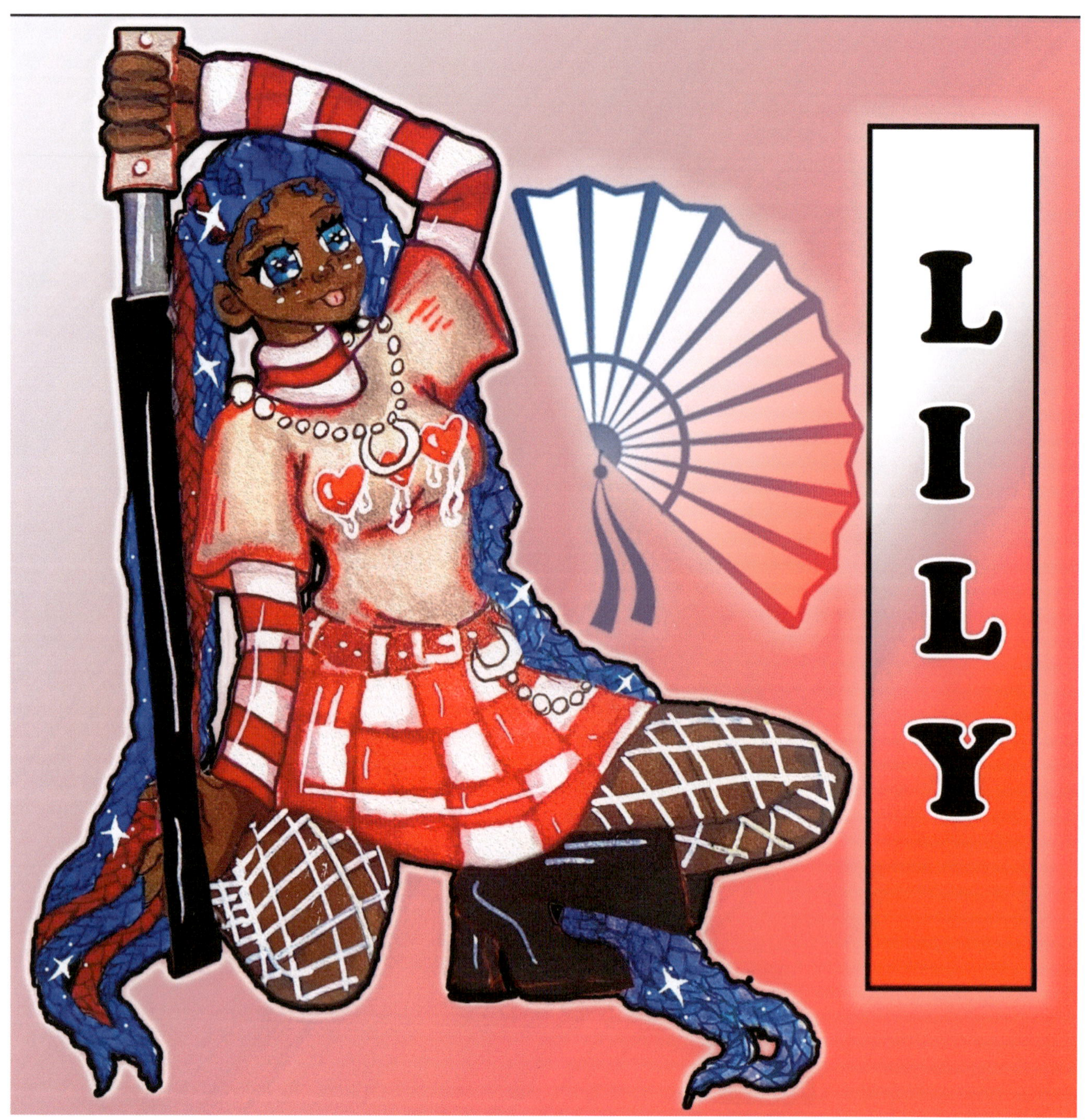
LILY

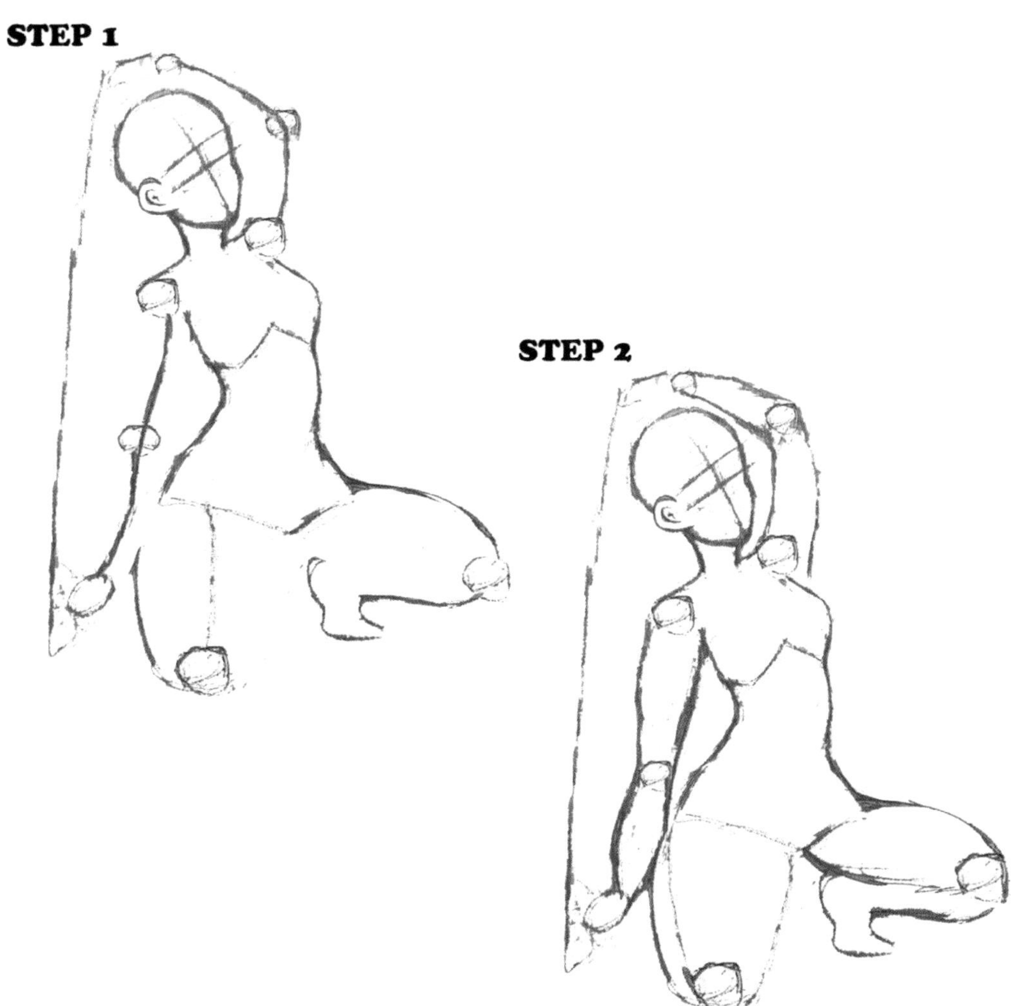
STEP 1
STEP 2

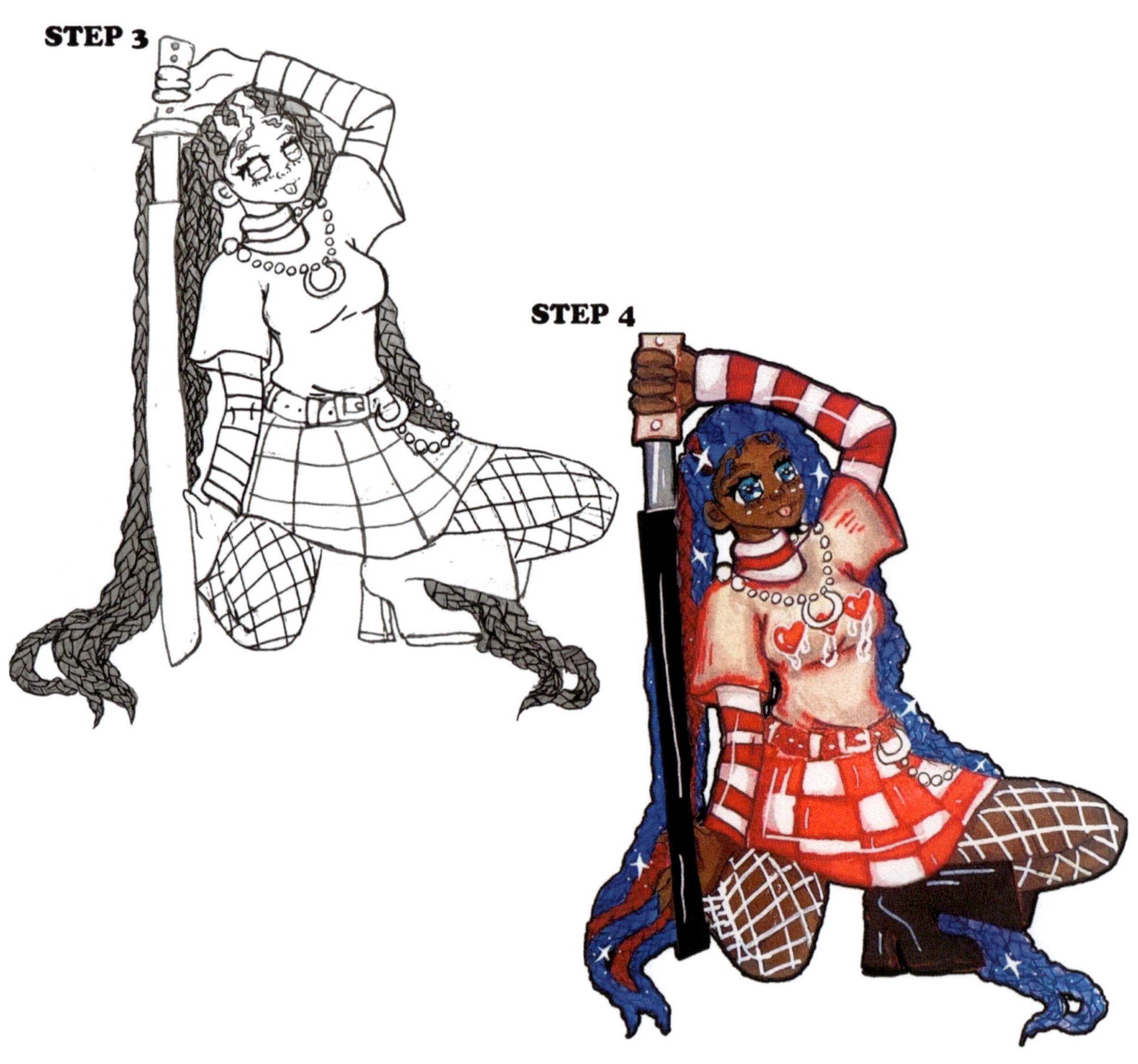
STEP 3
STEP 4

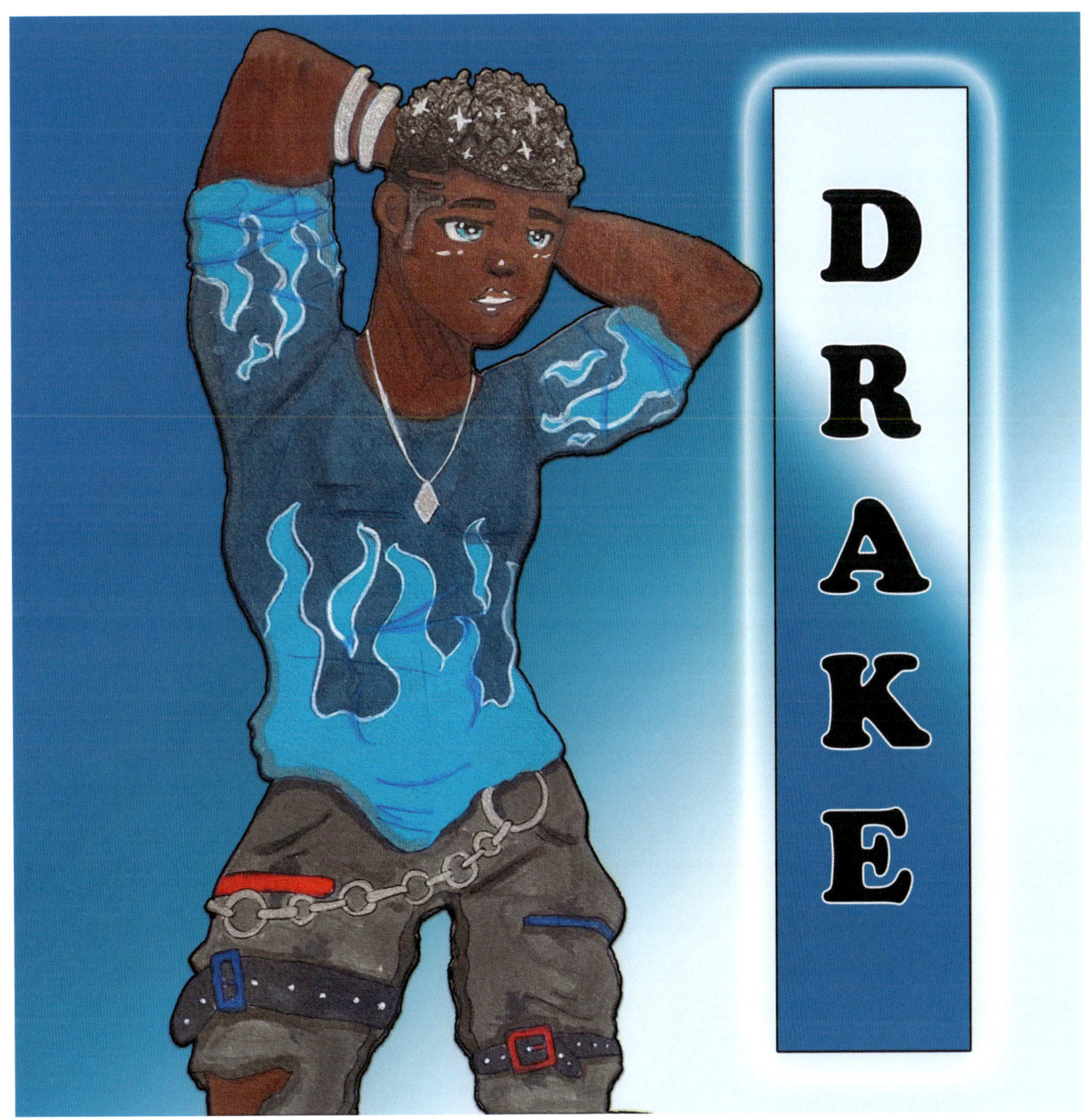
DRAKE

STEP 1

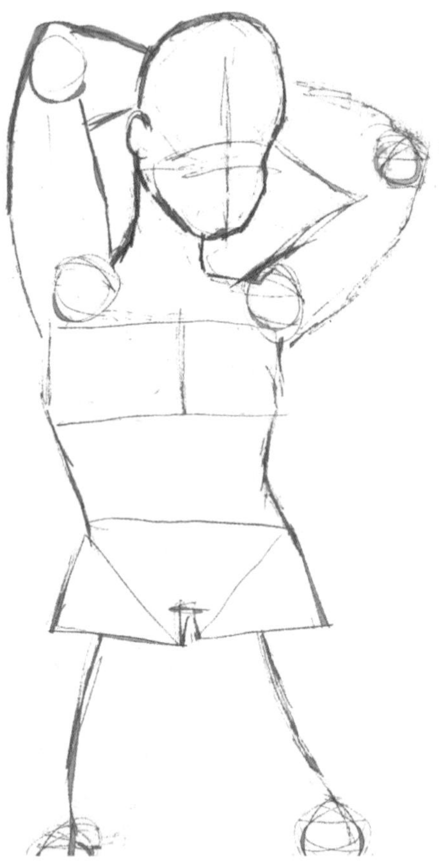

STEP 2

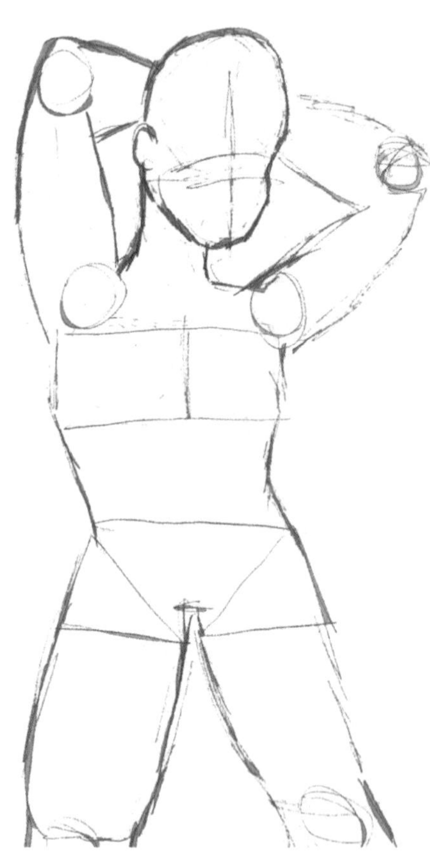

STEP 3

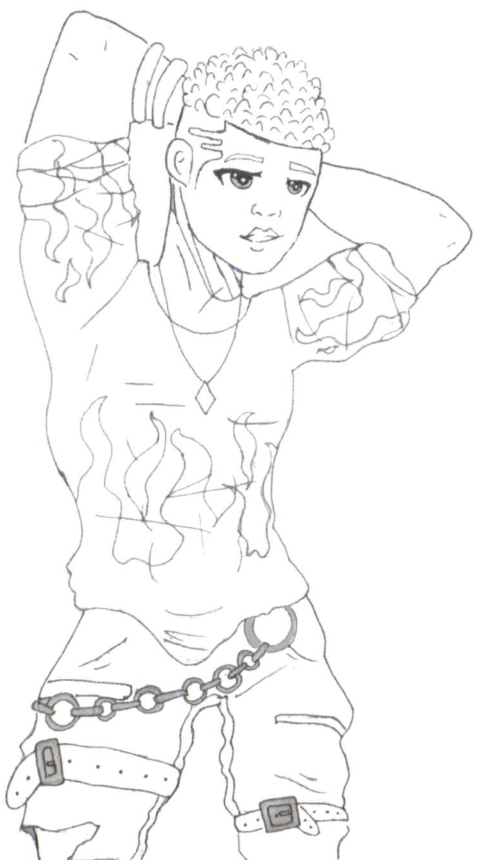

STEP 4

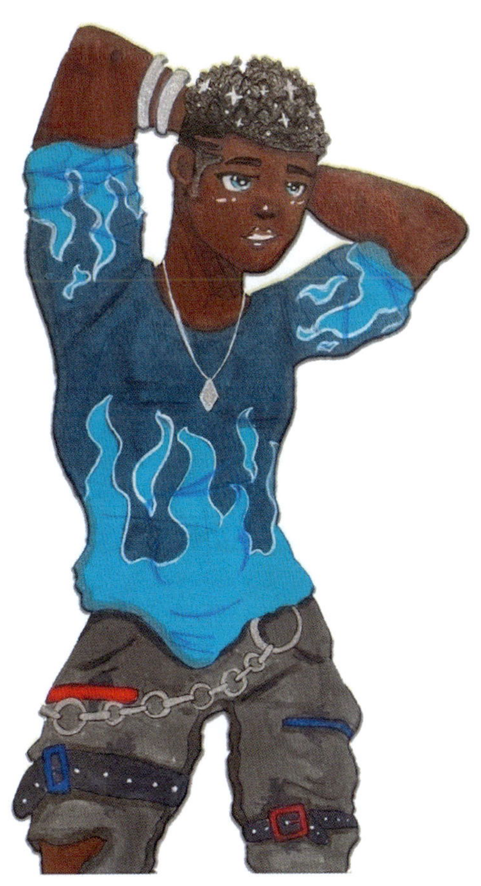

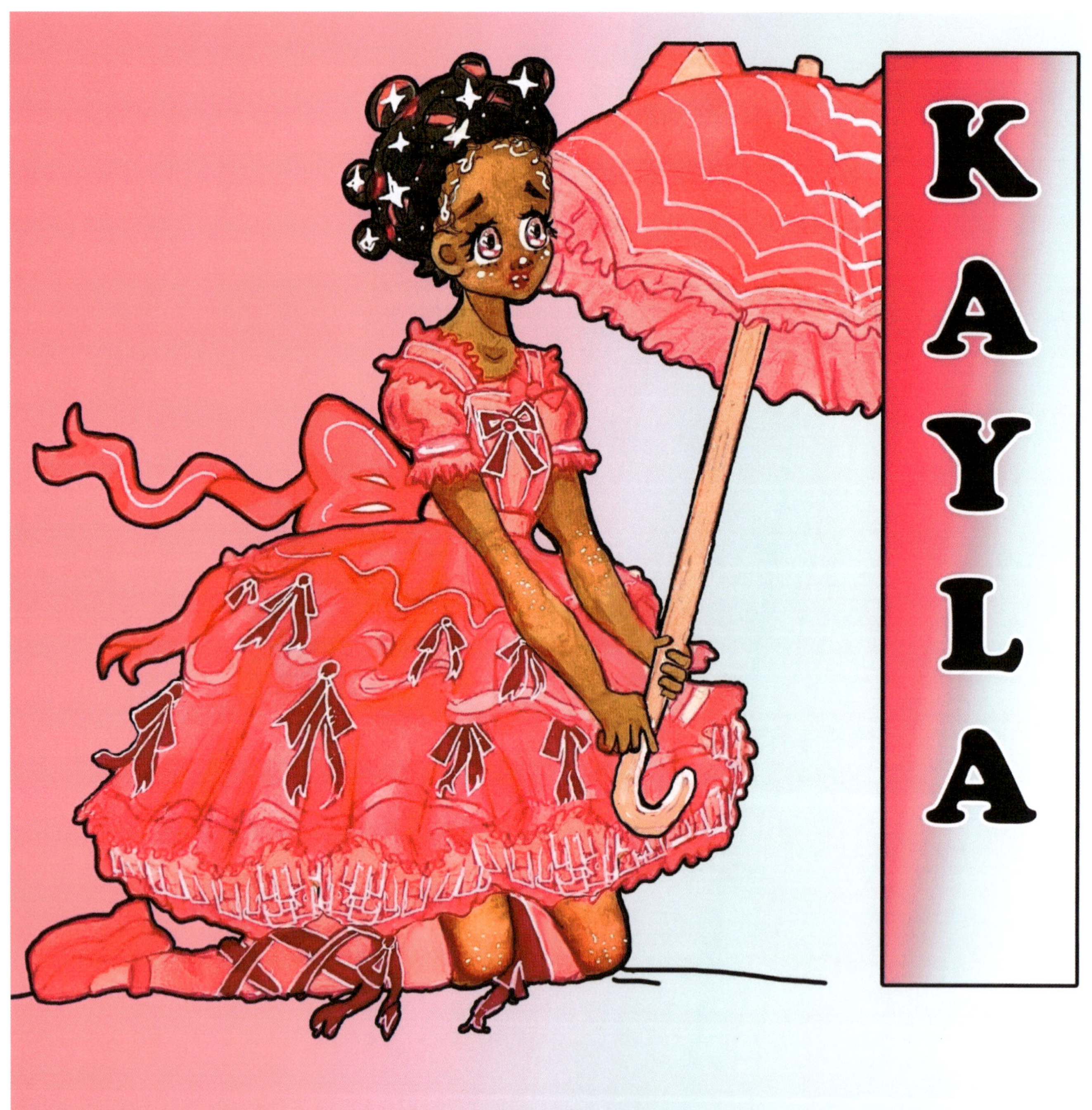
KAYLA

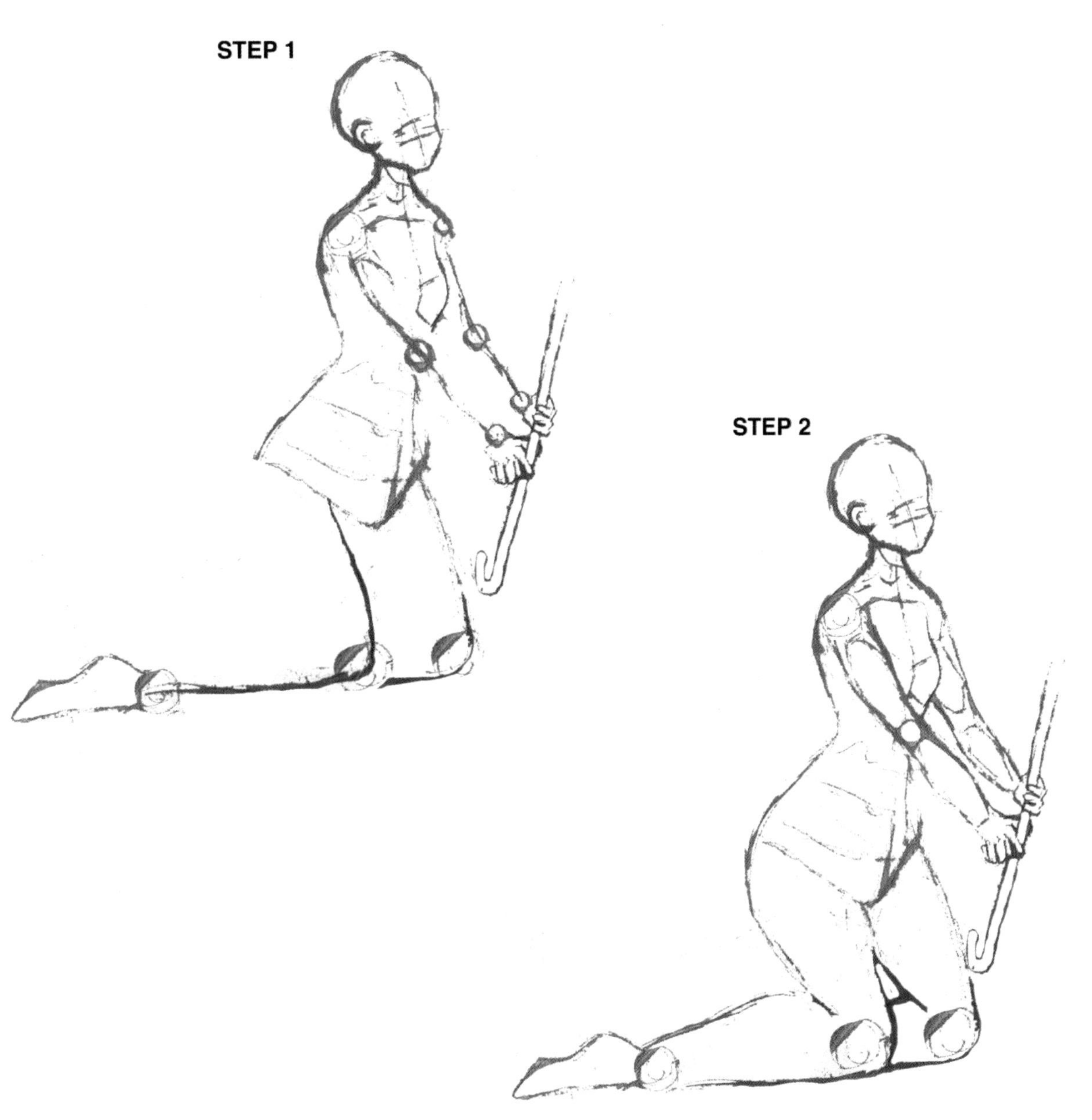
STEP 1
STEP 2

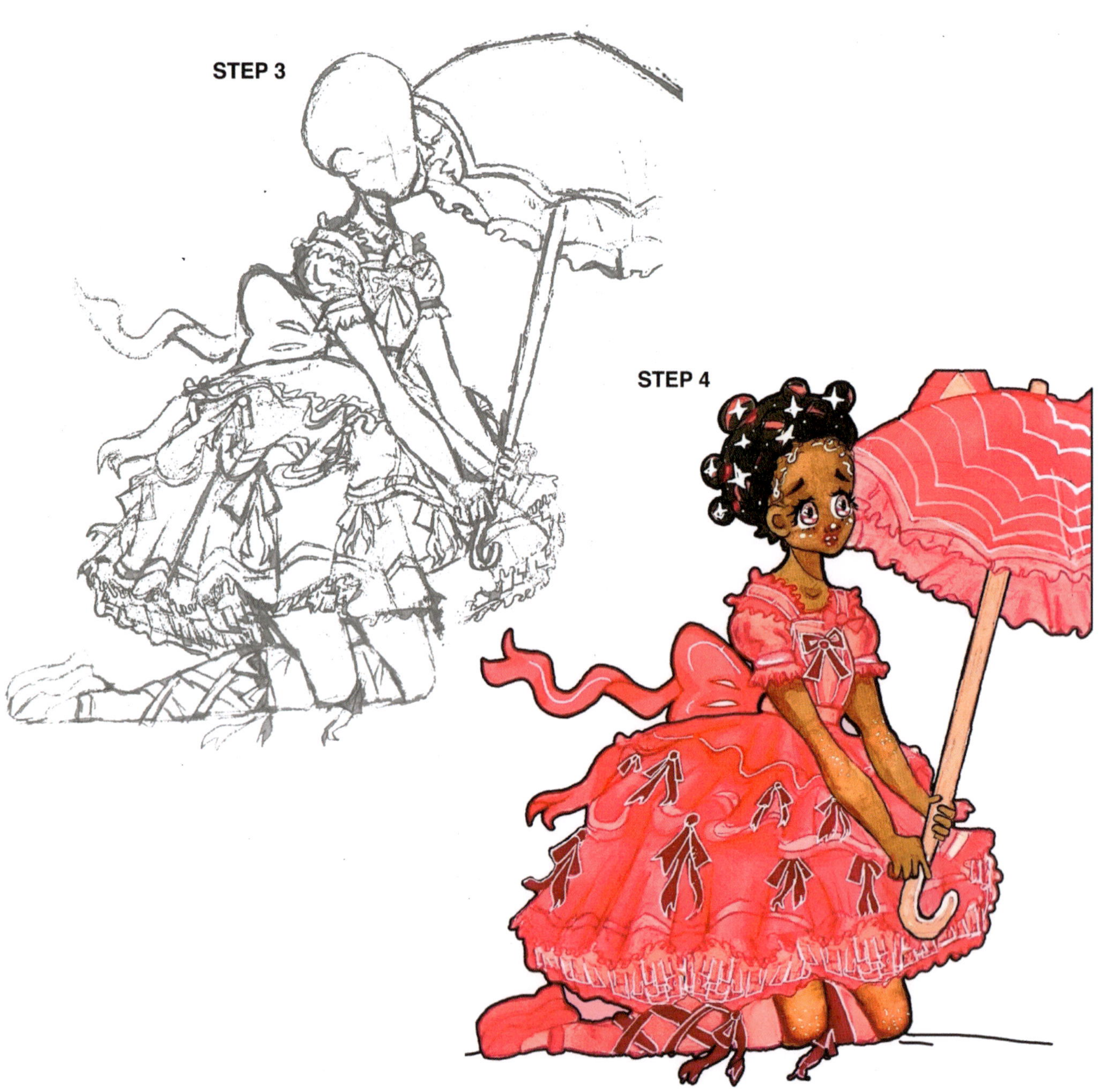
STEP 3
STEP 4

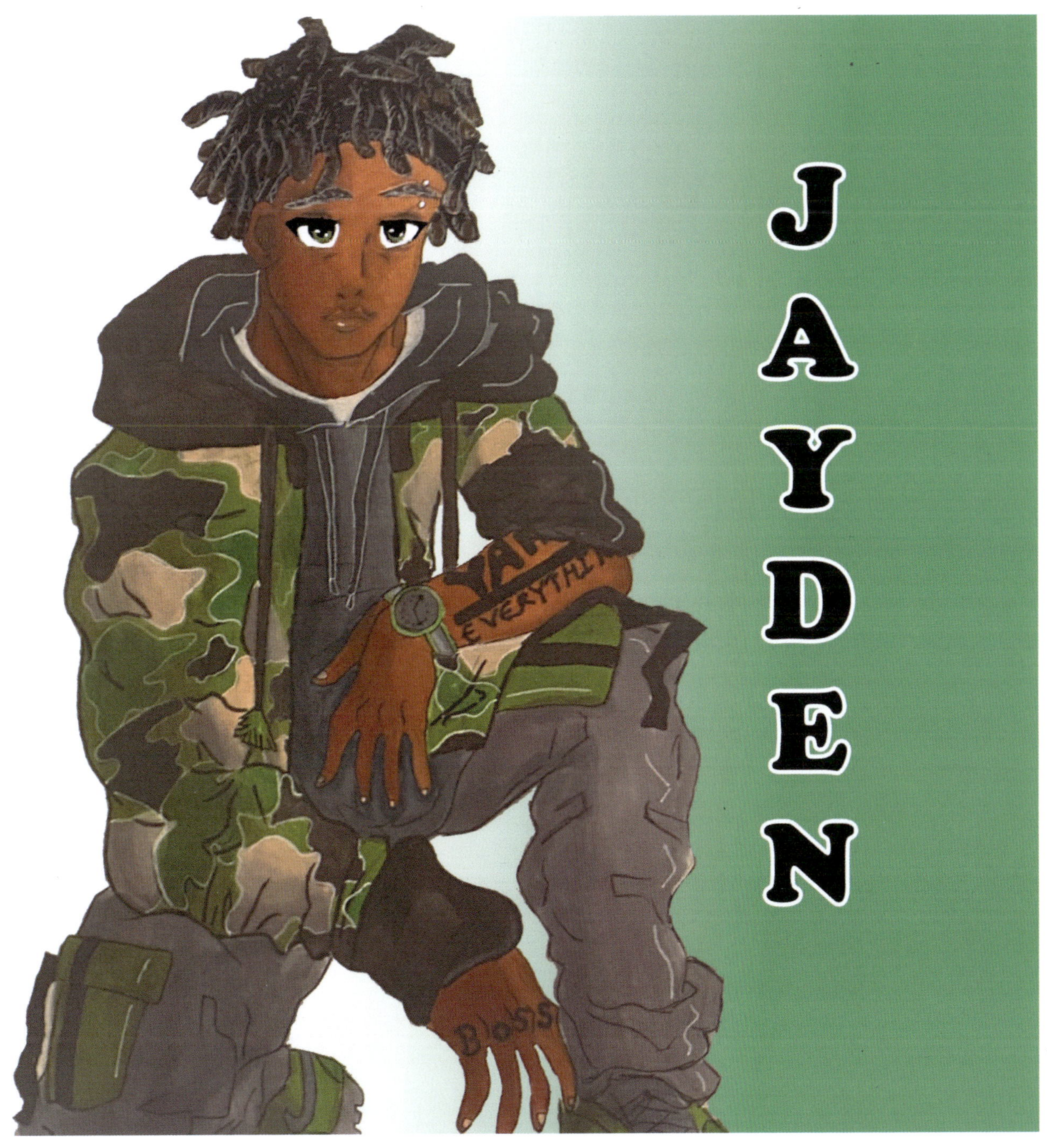
JAYDEN
EVERYTHI
BOSS

STEP 1

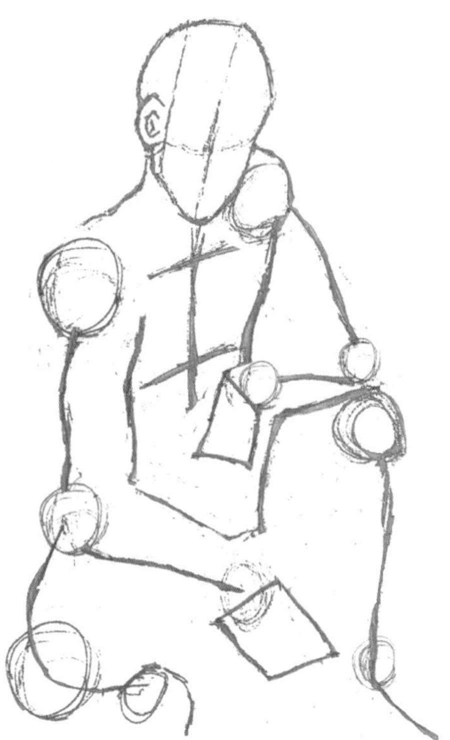

STEP 2

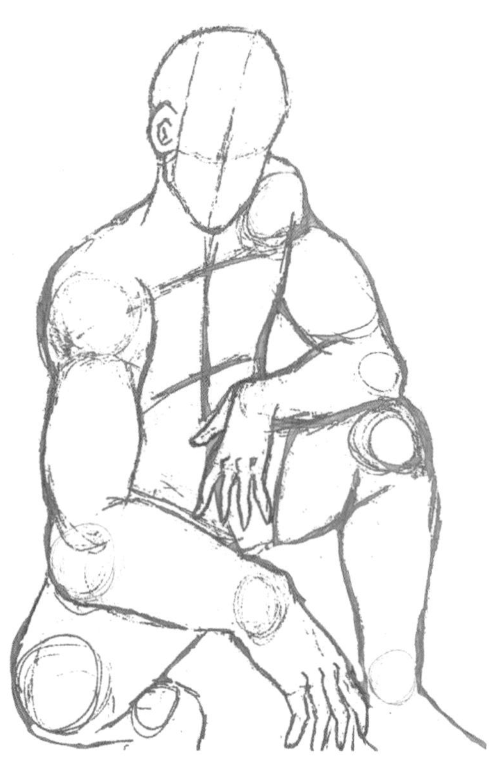

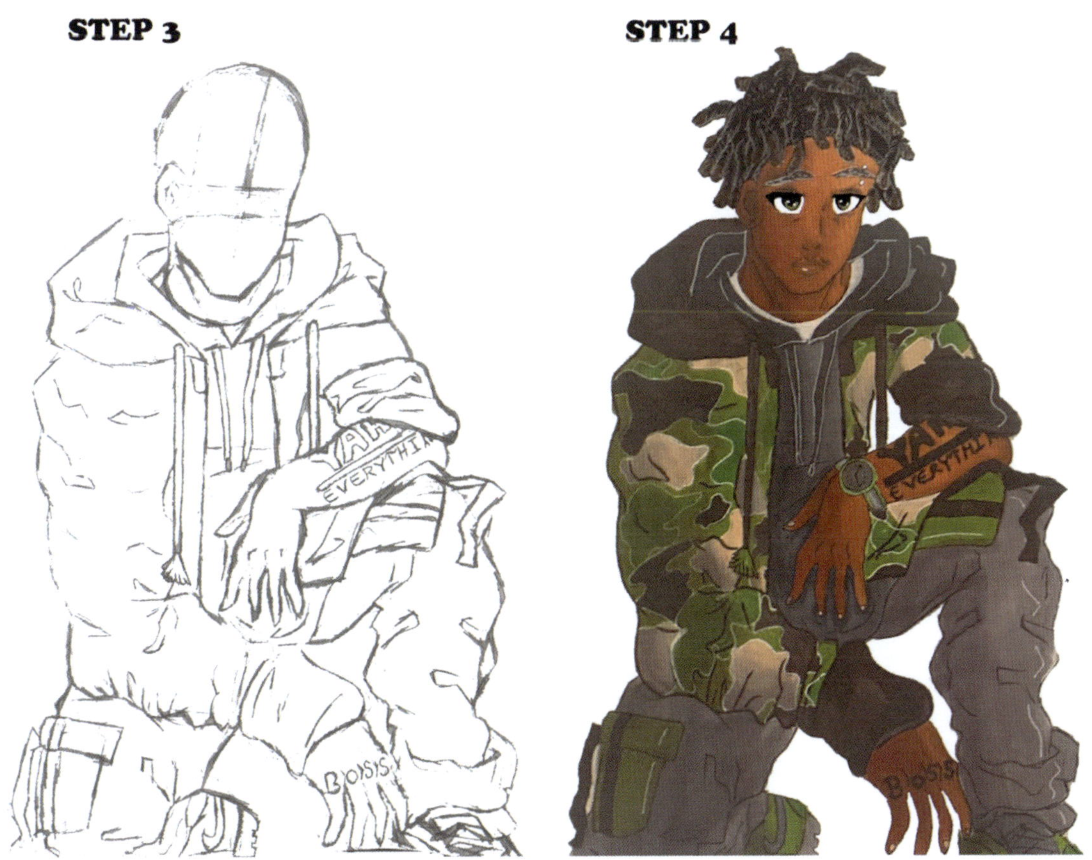
STEP 3
STEP 4

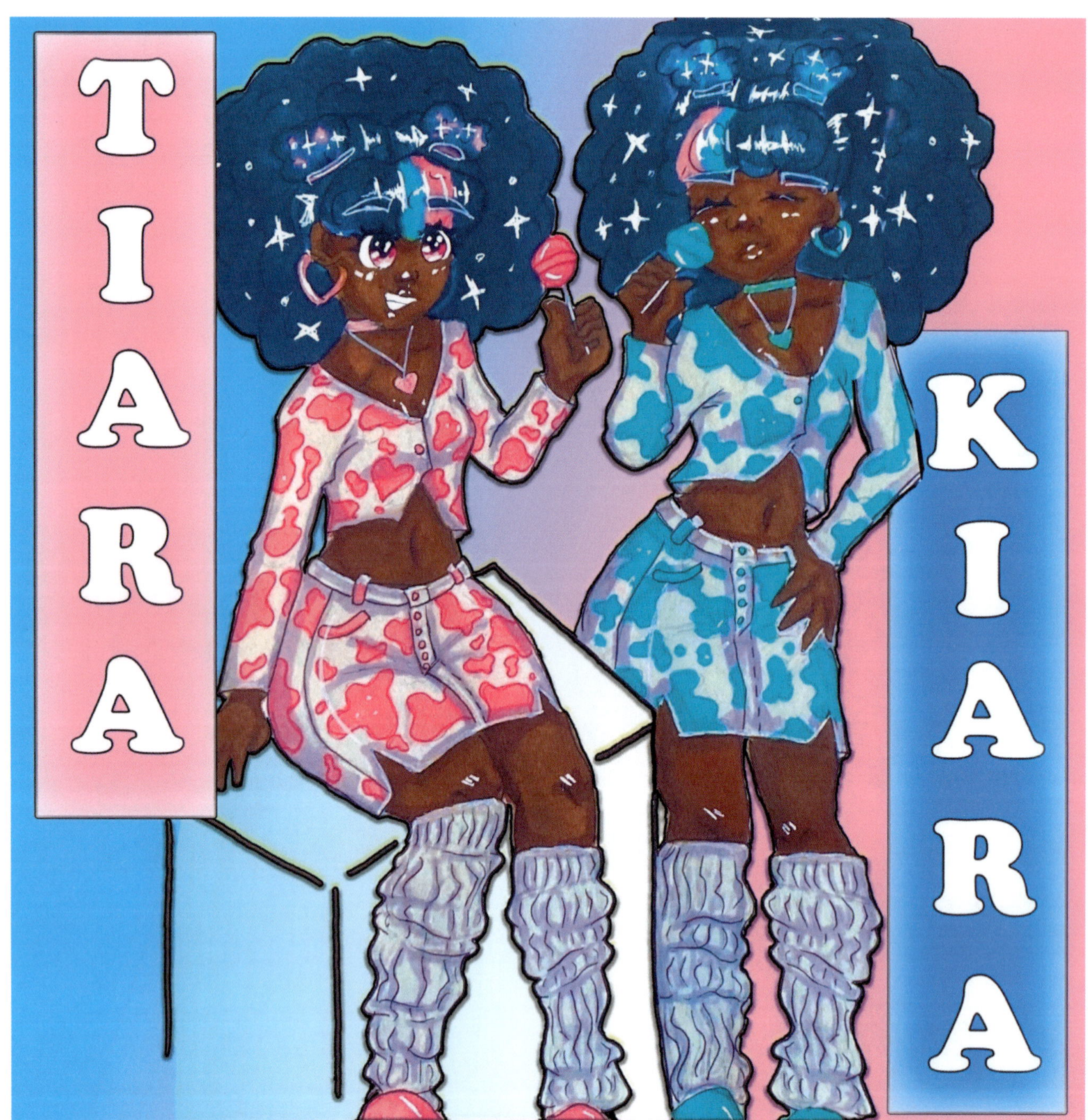
TIARA
KIARA

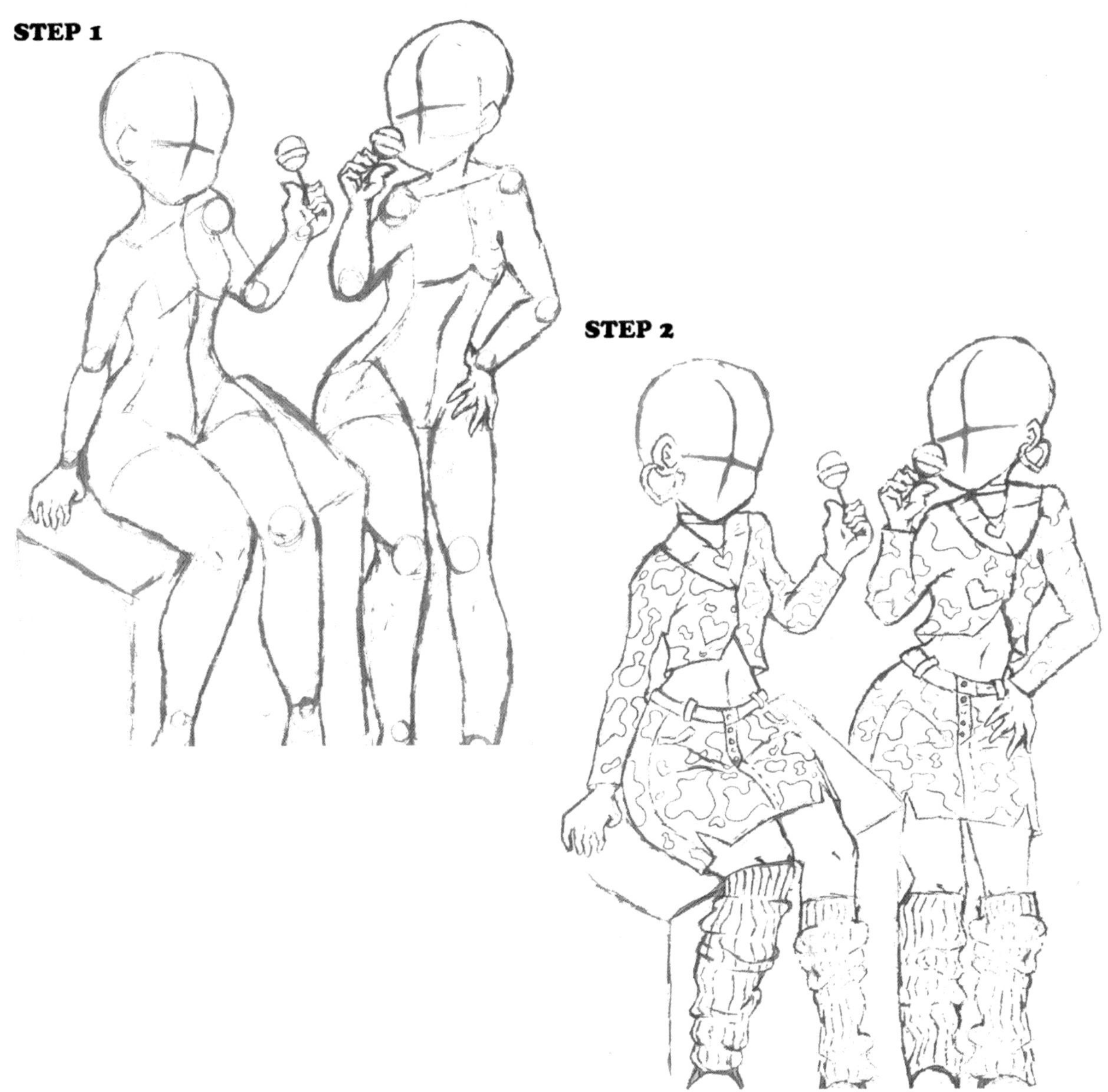
STEP 1
STEP 2

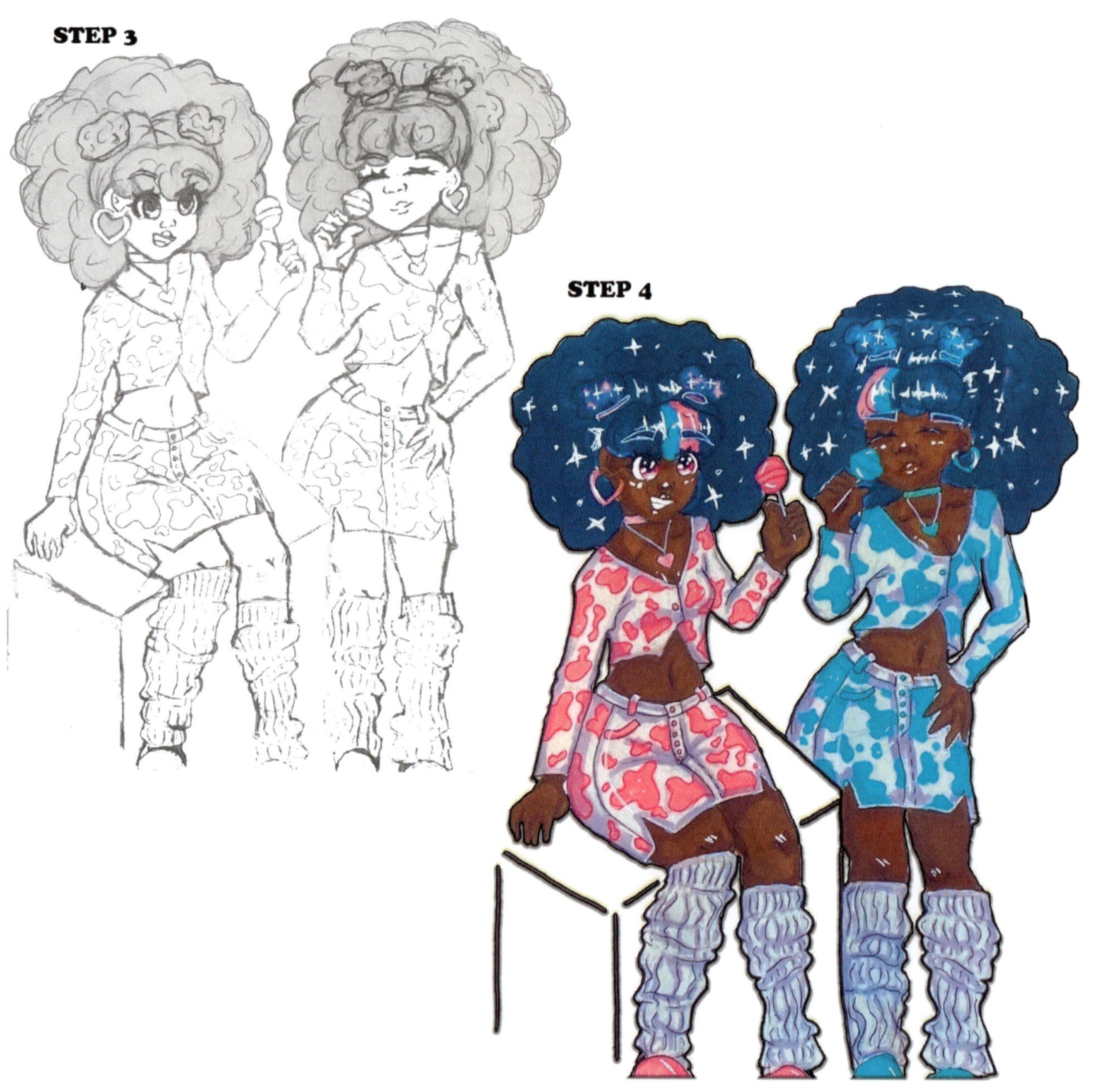
STEP 3
STEP 4

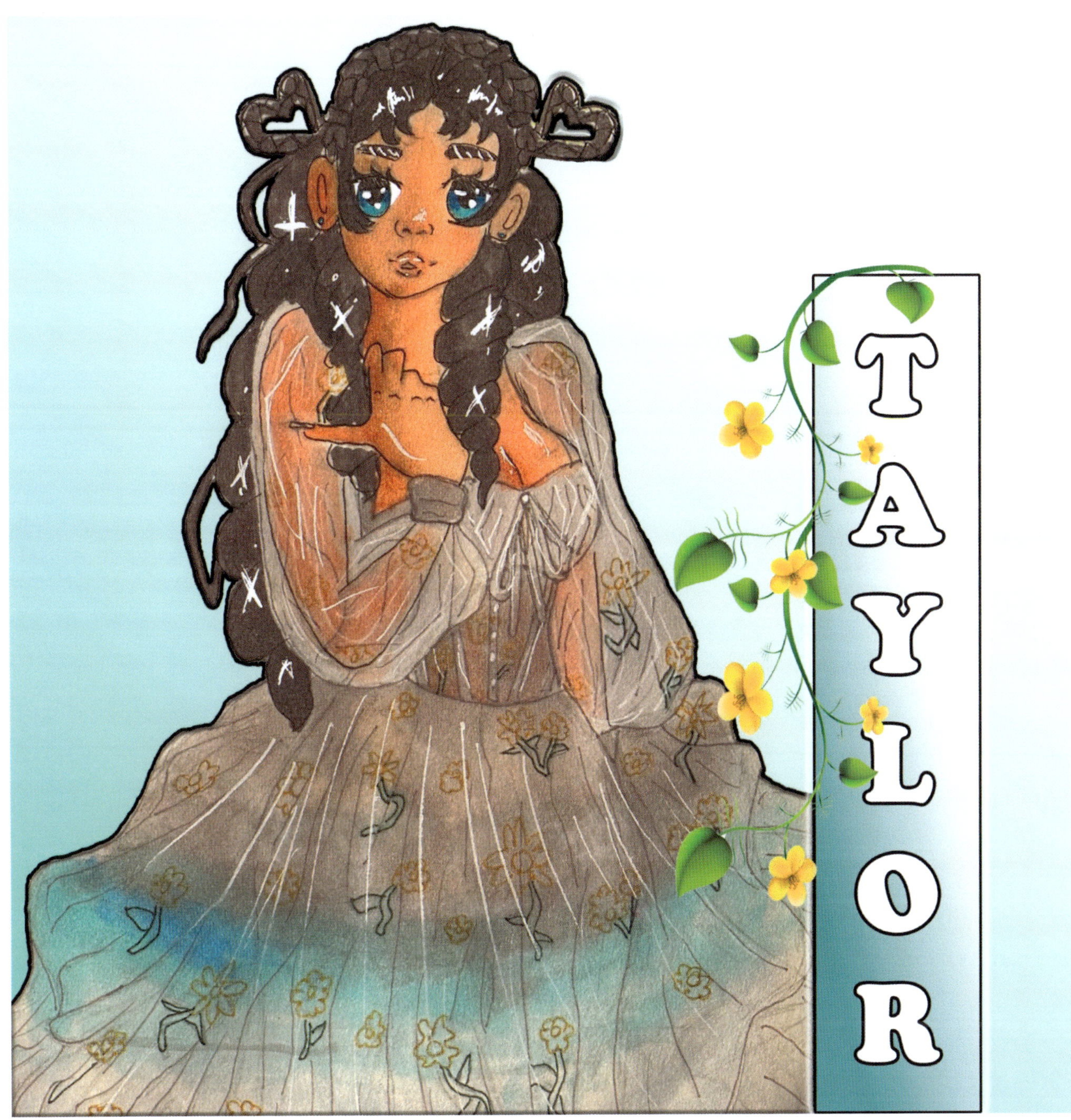
TAYLOR

STEP 1

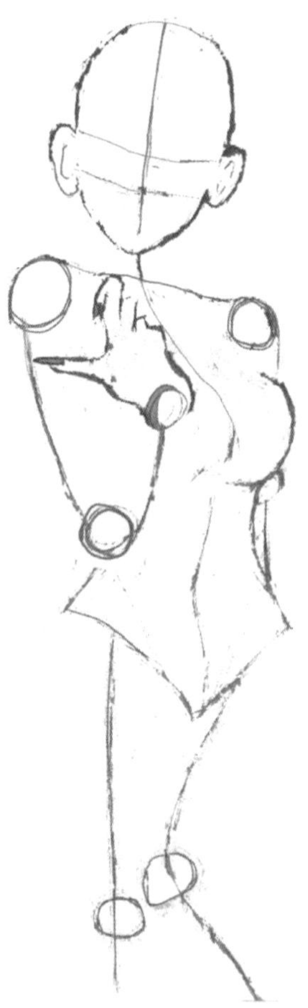

STEP 2

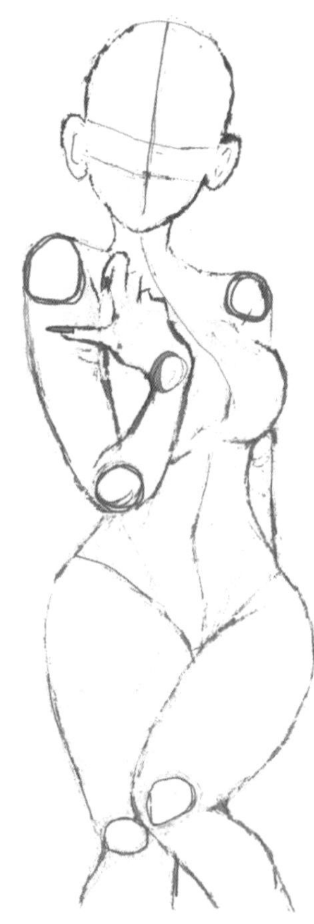

STEP 3

STEP 4

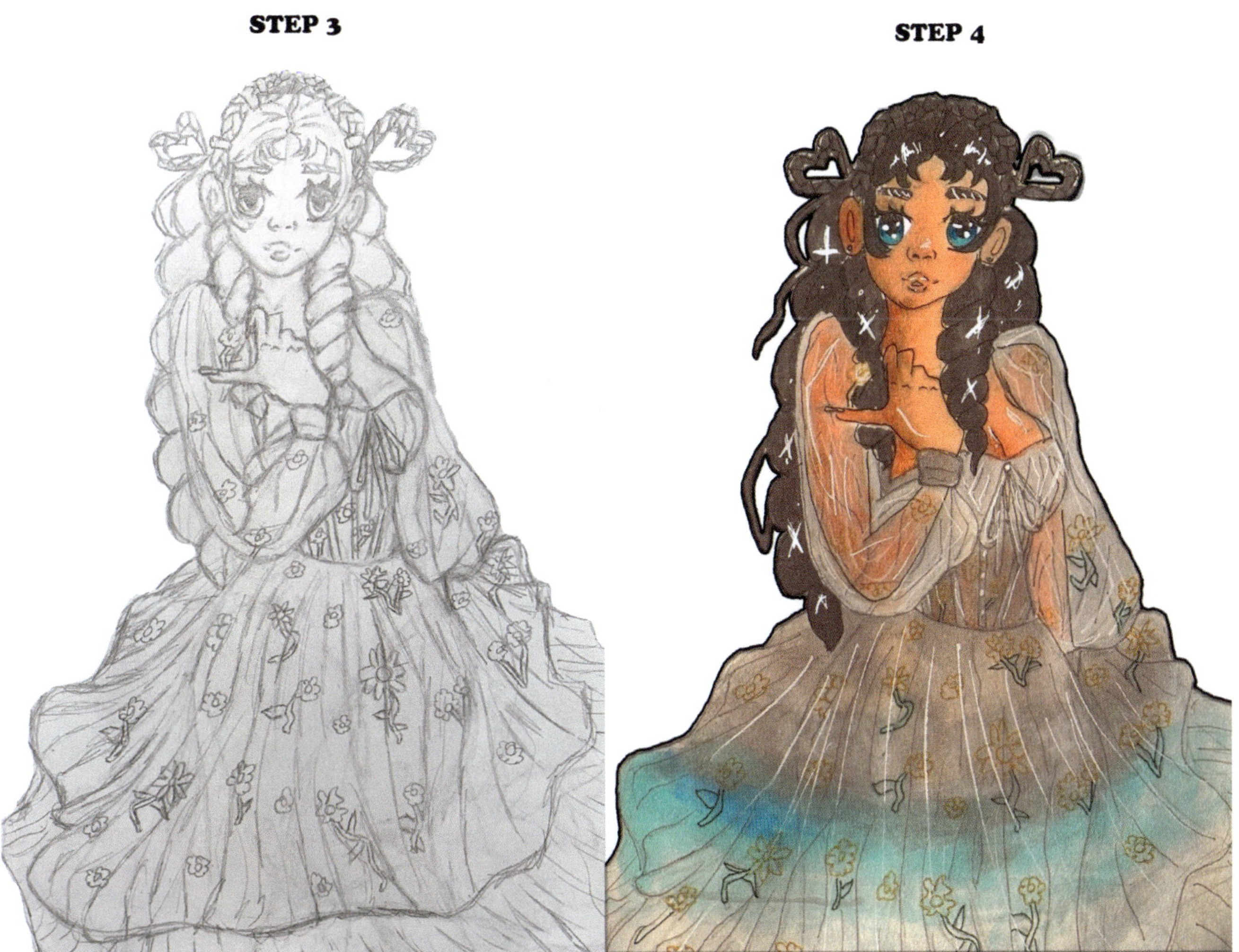

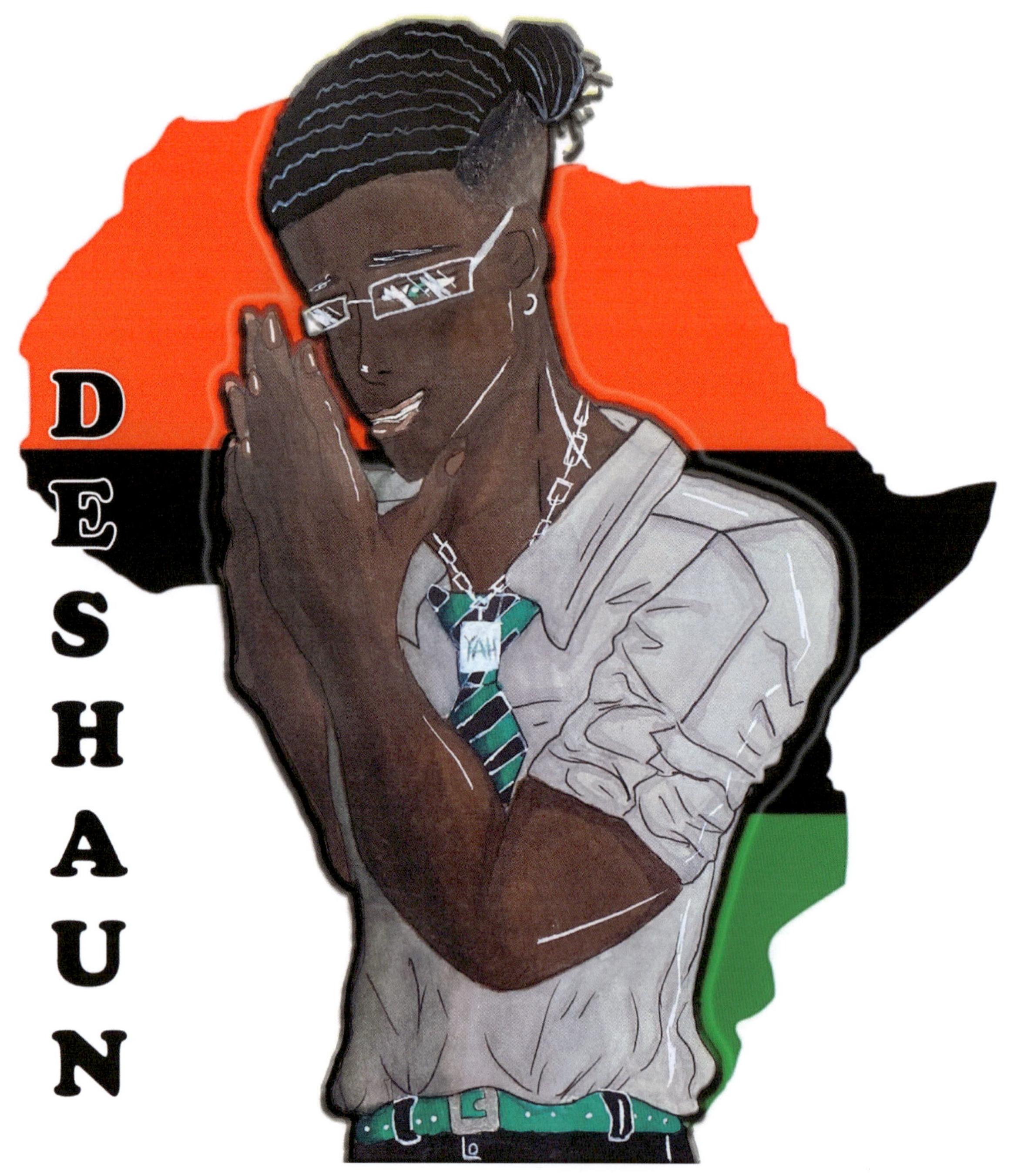
DESHAUN
YAH

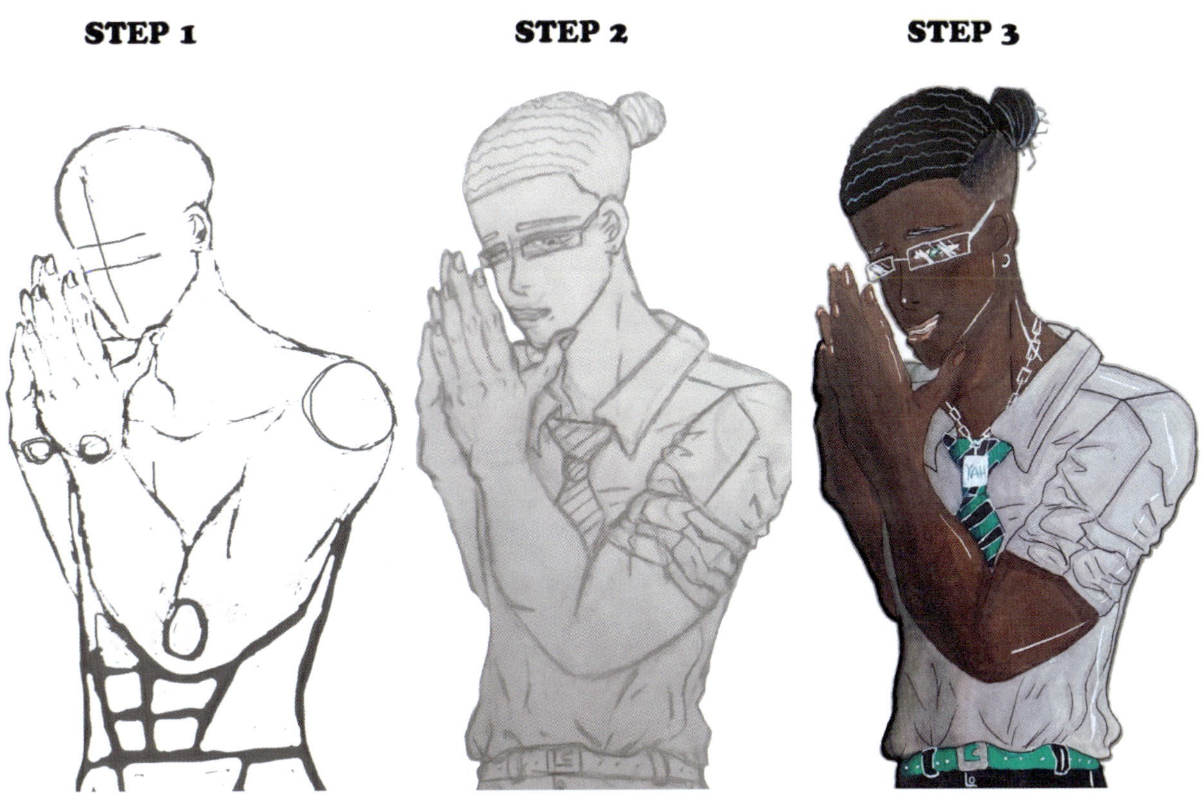
STEP 1
STEP 2
STEP 3

THE FUTURE IS IN YOUR HANDS!!!

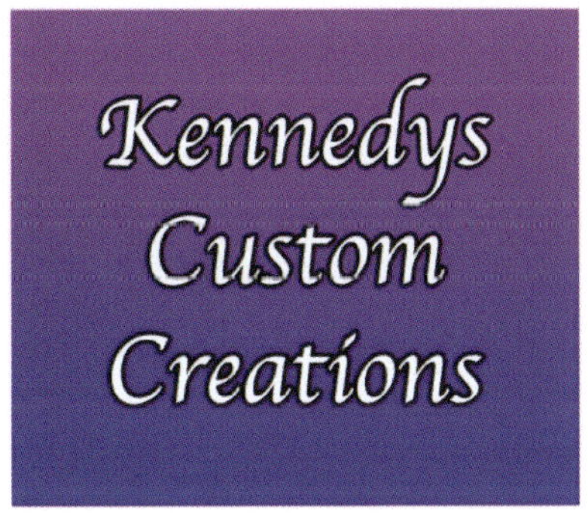

Visit my Youtube page at

Kennedys Custom Creations

Learn how to make sheer clothing, make wrinkles in clothes, and so much more!

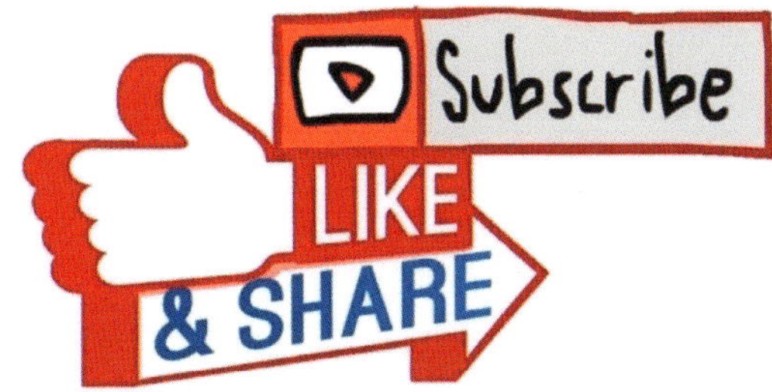

Printed in Great Britain
by Amazon